JAPANESE

VEGETARIAN
C O O K I N G

BY PATRICIA RICHFIELD

❋

THE CROSSING PRESS
FREEDOM, CA 95019

To Tian, Cominic, Cassian,
and Mitsuo, with love

Copyright © 1994 Patricia Richfield
Published in the U.S.A. by The Cossing Press in 1996,
First published in the U.K. by Judy Piatkus (Publishers) Ltd., London
Cover design by Victoria May
Photography by Gus Filgate
Food prepared by Jane Suthering
Calligraphy by Carl Rohrs
Line illustrations by Tony Masero
Printed in the U.S.A.
Second printing 1997

For information on bulk purchases or group discounts for this and other Crossing Press titles, please contact our Special Sales Manager at 800-777-1048.

Visit our Website on the Internet at: www.crossingpress.com

Library of Congress Cataloging-in-Publication Data

Richfield, Patricia.
    Japanese vegetarian cooking / Patricia Richfield.
      p. cm.
    Includes index.
    ISBN 0-89594-805-2
    1. Vegetarian cookery. 2. Cookery, Japanese. I. Title.
TX837.R485 1996
641.5'636'0952--dc20   96-4674
                              CIP

Identification of Photographs following page 88

Photo A Egg-drop Soup with Snow Peas (page 37), Clear Soup with Cucumber and Watercress (page 32), Soya Bean Paste Soup with Chunky Fried Bean Curd and Sweet Potatoes (page 42)

Photo B Green Pea Rice (page 50), Broccoli Salad with Seasame Dressing (page 142), Eggplant Grilled with Red Soya Bean Paste (page 102), Rice Wine and Sesame-Fried Carrots (page 117)

Photo C Tempura with all its accompaniments (pages 119-21)

Photo D Sticky Red Rice (page 48), Okra with Miso and Sake Sauce (page 112), Giant White Radish with Soya Bean Pastw Dressing (page 111)

Photo E Chilled Buckwheat Noodles (page 80), Chilled Giant Radish and Carrot Salad (page 140), Chilled Silken Tofu Pieces (page 86), Beansprout and Cucumber Salad with Horseradish Dressing (page 139)

Photo F Natto Udon Noodles (page 75), Japanese Squash Simmered in Rice Wine and Soy Sauce (page 112), Shiitake Mushrooms with Ginger and Seaweed (page 100) Spinach Rolls with Sesame Seeds (page 116)

Photo G Rice and Mushrooms (page 51), Asparagus Salad with KimiZu Dressing (page 141), Fried Soya Bean Curd Rolls Stuffed with Fresh Tofu and Vegetables (page 88), Simmered Whole Onions (page 110)

Photo H Vegetable Pancake (page 118), Lotus Root and Sweet Red Pepper Salad in Sake Dressing (page 142)

VEGANS

Dairy products are not a traditional part of the Japanese diet, and all the recipes in this book are suitable for vegans, except those marked Ⓥ.

CONTENTS

INTRODUCTION

The visual elegance, delicacy of flavor and sheer delicious-ness of Japanese food make it both a delight to the eye and a joy to eat. Add to this its high-fiber, low-calorie and low-fat content; its speed of cooking, which retains all the freshness of flavor as well as the high vitamin, mineral and other health-giving properties, and you have probably the finest and healthiest cuisine in the world.

Many Western diseases are now known to be diet related, and the fact that the Japanese suffer fewer heart diseases than we in the West, and have the longest life expectancy in the world—82 years for a female and 76 for a male—has been largely attributed to their diet, which must be the ideal cuisine for the health conscious.

With the ever-increasing interest in health and diet issues, increasing numbers of people are revising their Western diet, traditionally overloaded with artery-clogging, cholesterol-rich fats, high in sugars and calories, low in fiber and mostly over-cooked so that many of the vitamins and minerals are destroyed or discarded with the cooking water. In this context Japanese food has come as a revelation and Japanese food shops, restau-rants and supermarkets are flourishing, especially in the United States, as never before.

Creatures without feet have my love
And likewise do those with two feet
And those with four feet I love
And those too with many feet.

THE BUDDHA (566-486 B.C.)

THE JAPANESE VEGETARIAN TRADITION

Japan, unlike the West, has had a long and varied traditional vegetarian cuisine, evolving and perfecting itself over many centuries. A contributory factor has been the unusually wide variety of fruits, vegetables and edible fungi which flourish across her varied climates ranging from the sub-tropical in the south, where pineapples, sugar cane and watermelons are grown, to the temperate in the north, where long harsh winters can keep wheat fields and pastures under snow for months on end.

No part of Japan is far from the sea and an abundance of various seaweeds, with their delightful, fresh seafood taste and amazing nutritional value, have traditionally been harvested. Seaweeds contain all the nutrients required by human beings, including calcium and iron, as well as protein, essential trace elements and an abundance of vitamins including the elusive (for vegans) vitamin B^{12}. Soy bean curd, *tofu*, is rich in calcium and vitamin B^{12} and has about a 38 percent protein content, equal to that of beef; it was the principal source of protein in Japan until quite recently. With the addition of grains and rice you have the basis of the traditional Japanese cuisine. A little fish was sometimes added, or occasionally a bird, rabbit or even wild boar was caught, but very little meat was eaten right up to the *Meiji* era, 1869-1911. A third-century Chinese document reveals that in Japan "in winter as in summer the people live on vegetables," and an Elizabethan traveler observed "They delight not much in flesh, but live for the most part with herbs, fish, barley, and rice."

In about 500 A.D. Buddhism arrived in Japan and has happily co-existed alongside the indigenous Shintoism to this day. To complement Buddhist ethics of love and respect for all living creatures, fish and meat were avoided by the monks, nuns and lay followers. The simple vegetarian diet of this era is known as *kosei shojin.*

Let him extend unboundedly
His heart to every living thing.

THE BUDDHA (566-486 B.C.)

In the Kamakura era, 1185-1333, Buddhism spread very widely throughout Japan and the vegetarian cuisine of this era, *shojin ryori*, became further enriched by the addition of diverse regional produce and cooking methods.

During the *Edo* period, 1603-1861, the Zen Buddhist influence enjoyed a flowering, at which time the court cuisine in Kyoto, the ancient capital of Japan, became vegetarian. Even today Kyoto is famed for its vegetarian specialties. The Zen-inspired court cuisine aspired to satisfy the taste, stomach, eye and spirit, and with breathtaking artistic and culinary innovation, the great vegetarian chefs of the imperial court transformed the humble vegetable into unsurpassed visual and edible masterpieces, exquisite in taste, texture, form and color, set jewel-like against backgrounds of lustrous lacquered and gilded dishes and bowls.

From the plain rice, crunchy salt pickles, rustic soups and simple vegetable dishes of the farmers and peasants, to the fantastically sculptured forms and exquisitely garnished delicacies prepared for the Emperor and his court, Japan has provided us with a vegetarian cuisine of exceptional variety and excellence.

COOKING AND DINING JAPANESE STYLE

SETTING THE SCENE

. . . And on our road
The sweet-scented
Orange tree in bloom.

EMPEROR OJIN (REIGNED 270-312)

It is always exhilarating to cycle around the countryside in Japan, out across the wide earth ridges that cut through and divide the frog-croaking paddy fields, the most brilliant of greens in the spring, from where a tall white crane can suddenly rise and head towards far-off horizons, symbolizing to the Japanese the heights to which the human spirit can soar.

Solitary bird.
Racing the oncoming night
To distant mountains.

THE AUTHOR

The country lanes still have their old unused stone lanterns, and wind past groups of mandarin orange and persimmon trees hung with glossy apricot-orange fruits that seem lit up in the sun; past small *Shinto* shrines where the young children have always been allowed to noisily laugh and play, and old wooden farmhouses where swathes and bunches of fruits and vegetables decoratively festoon the depths of their shady verandas, gently drying into soft glowing colors before being preserved or pickled.

My parents-in-law live in a typical traditional farmhouse in the Japanese countryside. It is basically a large, strong wooden frame, raised up from the ground on posts, and roofed in decorative blue-grey glazed ceramic tiles. The ceilings are of warmly matured, unpainted wood. The walls and sliding doors are made of fragile rice paper panels, *shoji,* which let in a softly diffused day-light. The dining room *shoji* opens on to a wooden verandah with steps leading down to a small formal Japanese garden.

Since recent rain,
Moss is greener than ever.
BASHO (1644-1694)

The garden is lovingly tended by Taisuke, my father in-law, and has large, strategically placed stones clad in deep green vel-vet moss; rich luxuriant ferns; small smooth, shiny black pebbles collected from a river and arranged to look vaguely river-like with emerald-green mossy, banks; symmetrically shaped and clipped evergreen cedars; dwarf maple trees, their cool summer green flaring into autumnal oranges and scarlet; and flowering camellias with glossy, rich green leaves and glorious blossoms—a harmonious private sanctuary in which to contemplate "life, the universe and everything." A productive kitchen garden pro-vides a year-long succession of vegetables and salads. Bamboo shoots and varieties of wild mushrooms are gathered from near-by mountains. A paddy field beside the house gives a year's sup-ply of rice. Other paddy fields, shady pine groves, small lakes with lotus and water lilies, vegetable fields and occasional farm houses extend in all directions to the mountains clothed in ever-green pines, bamboo thickets, wild wisteria and azaleas. Beyond is the rocky coastline edged with a few windblown pines, and the sea with its scattering of tiny volcanic islands, some waving delicate fronds of bamboo grass.

Full autumn moon.
Pine-tree shadow
On the tatami.

KIKAKU (1661-1707)

The floors of the house, as in almost all Japanese houses and even council flats, are covered in the traditional thick rice-straw mats, *tatami*, which always seem to retain the fragrance of freshly mown hay. They are hand-woven in blocks of about three feet by six feet (calculated centuries ago to be a comfortable size to lie down on) by adding layer upon layer of thin rice-straw strands, until they are at least two inches thick. The deep *tatami* cover every floor and insulate the house, making the floors feel warm and comfortable to sit or lie on, and slightly springy to walk on. Shoes are always removed before stepping on to *tatami* whether in a restaurant or house, as apart from bringing in the outside dirt, they would also fray the woven straw. In most houses shoes are removed in the entrance hall, *genkan*, where several pairs of soft slippers are kept for guests as well as occupants. The custom of removing shoes had been so ingrained that in 1870, the passengers on the first train to run in Japan from Tokyo to Yokohama all arrived at their destination barefoot, having left the platform at Tokyo station covered in rows of neatly placed sandals and shoes.

On arriving home in the evening almost all Japanese take a daily bath before the evening meal, lathering themselves outside the bath-tub, *oforu*, and rinsing off with buckets and bowls on to the tiled floor in which there is a drainage plug. The main purpose of taking a bath in Japan seems to be rest and relaxation. Only when they are absolutely clean and rinsed do they climb into the bath-tub, which is about four feet deep. Here they sit upright, immersed up to the neck in hot, almost scalding, clean water, virtually floating, resting and soothing tired limbs, joints and brains. After the bath a clean *yukata* is put on—a simple cotton housecoat, padded in winter and printed in a beautiful blue and white traditional Japanese design. Clean, warm, comfortable, refreshed and relaxed, they can now begin the evening meal.

The formal dining and entertaining room at my parents-in-law's house is typical of those found in most Japanese homes. It is classically simple with the minimum of furniture, the main feature being a long, low, highly polished mahogany dining table which looks more like an elongated coffee table as there are no dining chairs. Before each meal is served, large square cushions, *zabuton*, are placed around it on the *tatami* flooring for the diners to sit or kneel on. The family shrine, *butsudan*, with its shiny lacquered doors, containing a gilded Buddha, Shinto artifacts and family relics, is housed in an alcove. A long, faded-looking scroll painting, *kakemono*, with a text written in Japanese calligraphy hangs on one wall. Beneath it, slightly raised up from the floor, stands an elegant ceramic flower vase containing, maybe, a single spray of plum or cherry blossom or white orchids, according to the season. This is arranged in the stunningly simple Zen-inspired tradition of *ikebana*, Japanese flower arranging, by my mother-in-law, Nobuko. Here the extended family or guests are entertained at New Year or any other celebratory occasion.

On a sunny summer's day it is very pleasant to sit here, or on the adjoining verandah, with a drink and a book or with some guests, the sliding rice paper panels fully opened to the birdsong and warm summer breezes or even completely removed so that the room, verandah and formal Japanese garden have become one.

Everyday family meals are eaten in a more informal dining/living room. Here the cushions are placed on L-shaped, legless chairs with padded back rests to provide more relaxation and comfort. In winter the square dining table is covered with a very thick, padded tablecloth, *kotatsu*, which extends out over the diners' laps, snugly covering them to just above the waist like a warm duvet. Underneath the table nestles a small electric heater. Traditionally this was a clay pot filled with hot charcoals. When the snow is piled high outside and the wind is rattling the wooden shutters, it is a uniquely delicious sensation to enjoy a leisurely meal, chat or watch television while cozily toasting one's feet under the table.

AFFINITY WITH NATURE

The Zen Buddhist and Shinto religions harmoniously co-exist in Japan and their influence pervades every aspect of Japanese culture, evoking a spiritual rapport in the Japanese soul to nature and the countryside. Pilgrimages to locations or events of awe-inspiring natural beauty have always held significance for Japanese of all ages.

Mountain mist.
Torches dropped
As the clouds grow red.
SHIRAO (1735-1792)

Climbing Mount Fuji at night to view the sunrise from the rim of its crater is as enthusiastically undertaken today as when this *haiku* was written two hundred years ago. Fuji is not difficult to climb and the six- to eight-hour ascent is begun in the early evening so as to reach the summit before sunrise. After darkness has fallen, the firefly lights of the hikers can be seen, magically illuminating the mountain as they climb up to view the spectacular event.

The full moon is a symbol of enlightenment to Buddhists and contemplating the full autumn moon, especially when it is reflected in water, is sacred ritual. The greater the turbulence of the water, the more indistinct the reflection. Only the calmest water can reflect the celestial image perfectly. Specially positioned moon-viewing rooms or verandas were built into country residences or temples so that the full autumn moon with its reflection in a pond or lake is perfectly positioned before the viewer.

Beneath the cherry trees
There are no strangers.
ISSA (1763-1827)

The mass pilgrimage to view the cherry blossoms is incredibly popular. During my first spring in Japan I was surprised when one of the main news stories, headlined along with all the political and international news, was that the cherry blossoms were at their peak on that particular day. This most eagerly awaited item of news sends the Japanese in their hundreds of thousands to merrily picnic off dainty morsels, quaff copious quantities of *sake* and even sing beneath the pink and perfumed boughs. The blossoms are often illuminated at night and the revels can continue until dawn. Perhaps the most spectacular of the many cherry groves in Japan are those of the Yoshino mountains where over 100,000 blossom-laden trees display their short-lived magnificence, with the slightest breeze enveloping the happy revelers in a swirling, pink confetti haze.

Affinity with nature is also expressed in the choice and presentation of Japanese food. As the seasons change, so the menu, garnish and even the decoration on the serving dishes and bowls are carefully selected to reflect the season. In winter thick warming soups, one-pot stews and dishes of winter mountain vegetables keep out the cold. In spring cherry blossoms garnish spring meals, where lightly cooked, fresh young vegetables take pride of place. In summer flowers appear beside chilled dishes served on beds of ice, to refresh and give relief from the heat and humidity. In autumn pumpkin and squashes, crisp fresh chestnuts and wild mushrooms are served with a few pieces of *takuan* pickle, the most brilliant of yellows, are served on a freshly fallen, red-gold leaf. (A deep red radicchio lettuce leaf looks almost as good.)

JAPANESE MEALS

At one sitting,
Two days' food
He tucks away.

BONCHO (?-1714)

Most Japanese start their day with a traditional hot breakfast of plain white rice, crunchy pickled vegetables and a steaming bowl of *miso* soup made from fermented soy bean paste, *miso*, and containing fried or plain soy bean curd, *tofu*, and a few vegetables. Sometimes a raw egg is cracked into the hot soup to be poached, or stirred into a bowl of hot rice with some crushed *nori* seaweed. A pot of green tea always accompanies the meal. Nowadays some busy working women and young people prefer coffee and toast. When in Japan I occasionally enjoy the popular "morning service" offered by some cafés and restaurants where, for little more than the price of a cup of coffee, you are served an "English" breakfast consisting of a boiled egg, slice of toast, muffin, butter, marmalade and as much freshly brewed coffee, served with jugs of cream and sugar, as you can drink.

Lunch is mostly eaten away from home as most working people in Japan commute. The Japanese equivalent to taking a couple of sandwiches to work in a paper bag is the lacquered lunchbox, *bento*. It is divided inside into two sections: one is for the rice, which can either be plain, or formed into rice balls or triangles, *onigiri,* which are either rolled in toasted sesame seeds or covered in paper-thin seaweed, nori; the other contains the *okazu*, which literally means "to accompany the rice." This is a selection of delicate savories such as a small rolled omelet, *tamago-yaki*, braised lotus root, *renkon*, or other vegetables and *sushi*, small shaped pieces of slightly sweet vinegared rice stuffed with salted cucumber, pickled plum or egg and garnished with savory morsels. Pickled vegetables, *tsuke-mono*, are always included.

Sushi bars are favorite places to lunch where many varieties of bite-sized *sushi* are continuously produced with speed and dexterity. Noodle bars are where you can enjoy, for example, a cheap and satisfying bowl of steaming thick *udon* noodles in a clear soup garnished with a slice of fried soy bean curd, *aburage*, and shredded spring onions.

Mid-afternoon tea, *oyatsu*, is either taken at home or in a restaurant, and is the time when the Japanese indulge in traditional types of sweet cakes and other desserts, which never form part of other meals. Traditional restaurants serve green tea and traditional Japanese confections such as sweet red beans in a sort of rice dumpling, *ohagi,* or the tiny, brilliantly colored, jewel-like morsels fashioned from *kanten* seaweed (agar-agar) and fruit, *awayukikan*. They are difficult to make and Japanese housewives leave their creation to experts, taking pride in knowing where to purchase good confections rather than make them themselves. Although these are artistically contrived, Westerners usually find them disappointing, and as they do not form part of Japanese meals I have not included them in this book. If you feel you must end a Japanese meal with a dessert, then fresh seasonal fruit is the most authentic.

Western-style tea and coffee shops are very popular in Japan, offering decor and refreshments of the most impressive quality. They are always filled in the afternoon with women shoppers who can usually select from a wide variety of special coffees and teas, and a superb continental patisserie of outstanding quality, often made on the premises by an expatriate French chef, or a Japanese trained in Europe and served on the most exquisite Western-style china.

The main meal of the day is the evening meal. There is no main dish as such, preceded by an hors d'oeuvre and followed by a dessert, but rather the meal is composed entirely of several small protein and vegetable dishes, which always include a thick or clear soup, rice and pickles. Occasionally fresh fruits, which at formal meals can be sculpted into fantastic forms, conclude the meal, but never sweet desserts.

WHAT TO DRINK WITH A JAPANESE MEAL

Instead of useless worrying
One should down
A bowl of rough sake.

OTOMO TABITO (665-731)

A companionable pot of Japanese green tea, *ocha,* which is frequently topped up with hot water and drunk throughout the meal from small, eggcup-sized bowls, accompanies most family or informal meals (see pages 151–2). Japanese fortified rice wine, s*ake,* which in the past accompanied only formal or celebratory meals, is drunk more frequently nowadays due to the increasing prosperity of the Japanese. *Sake* can accompany any main meal. It is decanted into a decorative porcelain flask which is immersed in hot water until it reaches blood heat, then drunk from small, flat, matching bowls while another flask is warming. Although traditionally drunk warm, it can also be served cold or iced.

There is much lively refilling of *sake* bowls during a Japanese meal as the vessels are so tiny. Japanese sensibility, however, prevents the drinker from refilling his own *sake* bowl. Instead he attends to his neighbors' requirements. Pouring your host some of his own *sake* will be rewarded by profuse thanks and many little bows of the head. It is the custom for a mouthful of *sake* to be drunk before any food is eaten, and occasionally chrysanthemum petals, which are thought to promote long life, are floated on top. When no more *sake* is required the *sake* bowl is simply turned upside down on the table. Nowadays whiskey, Japanese beer or a light Japanese wine are often drunk throughout a meal.

Umeshu, plum wine, can be drunk at any time, and I give a recipe for it on page 154.

The Japanese toast, equivalent to "cheers" or "here's health" is "*kanpai,*" which roughly translates as "emptying the *sake* bowl."

COOKING
JAPANESE-STYLE

It is surprising how many people are afraid to try their hand at authentic Japanese cooking, fearing that it involves laborious and lengthy procedures, or that there must involve some ancient mystique. The truth is that Japanese food is really very easy and quick to cook, and most recipes are far less complicated and time consuming and very often leave considerably less mess and washing up than many Western dishes. No complex cooking methods are employed; Japanese food is cooked in the same way as Western food by grilling, boiling, deep-frying or steaming. In fact Japanese kitchens are often rather small and less well equipped than their Western equivalents. Everything is cooked as lightly and quickly as possible to conserve the color, shape and natural freshness of flavors without the addition of heavy or overspiced sauces and seasonings. The typical, delicate and delicious Japanese flavors are obtained by the use of specific seasonings and a few uniquely Japanese ingredients, all of which are listed in the glossary on page 156. These are now readily available in this country, and once you have obtained what you need to cook your Japanese meal you will be surprised, and thrilled, to find that you can easily produce delicious, authentic Japanese meals with no more difficulty than you can an ordinary pasta dish.

Traditional Japanese knives, steamers, strainers, saucepans and other equipment are available in specialty stores, but their Western equivalents can be used with equal success. The only exception is the Japanese omelet pan, *tamago yoki nabe*. It is unique, being small and rectangular in shape, enabling you to make a perfect, rolled, straight-sided omelet with ease. Nonstick ones with wooden handles that are imported from Japan are no more expensive than an ordinary omelet pan.

If you can find a store which stocks traditional pots, tableware, frying pans and condiments, it will be a pleasurable experience checking out what's offered.

I have included a list of suppliers of Japanese foods on page 164.

SERVING A JAPANESE MEAL

Western food—
Every single plate
Is round!

ANON

So wrote a Japanese *haiku* poet in the last century when, on a visit to Paris, he was served his first Western meal. In complete contrast, a Japanese meal is served in several individual bowls and dishes in a variety of shapes and colors, such as small bowls with domed lids for soup, *shire mono*; tall lidded cups for savory steamed custards, *chawan mushi*; flat woven bamboo baskets for deep-fried vegetables, *tempura*; square wooden dishes with slatted bases to stand in ice for iced noodles, *zaru soba*; small delicate bowls for rice, *gohan;* deep capacious bowls for thick noodles, *udon*; small flat dishes for pickles, *tsuke mono*; and plates and dishes of every conceivable shape, some with separate sections for sauces or dips.

Japanese tableware is most frequently made of porcelain, glazed ceramic and plain or gilded lacquer. Wood and woven bamboo are also used. Nowadays imitation lacquer bowls and dishes of excellent design are popular for informal and restaurant meals. They are made of extremely tough, long-lasting plastic and are very practical, being virtually indestructible in use. I accidentally knocked a complete set of beautiful black and ochre, delicately gilded plastic soup bowls and lids from a high shelf onto a quarry-tiled kitchen floor—horror! Not one of them was broken, or even chipped!

Unlike the overloaded dinner plate of the West, Japanese foods are usually served separately rather than in combination so that their individual flavors and appearance can be fully appreciated. Each diner is served with his or her own set of chopsticks, bowls and dishes, carefully chosen for their form, and often their color, to harmonize with and complement the tiny, artistically arranged portions of food they contain. These place settings may be arranged on individual lacquer trays.

Attractively arranged and garnished Japanese food is set off to perfect advantage in Japanese tableware, but you can start off using Western dessert and soup bowls and small plates. Rice and noodle bowls are increasingly available in stores and are no more expensive than their Western equivalent.

Seeing a typical Japanese meal laid out with its array of variously shaped plates, dishes and bowls gives the impression that considerably more cooking has been involved than for a Western meal prepared for a similar number of people. This is not necessarily the case. A typical Japanese meal can consist of, say, four or five dishes such as rice, soup and two or three savory dishes, each charmingly served in its own bowl or dish with its complementary garnish. A typical Western meal can consist of a similar number of components such as, say, a main course, potatoes, vegetables, a stuffing and sauce or gravy. The fact that it is all heaped on to one plate doesn't necessarily indicate that less cooking was involved.

Serving your Japanese meal in a Western dining room will not look at all out of place as many Japanese houses and flats, especially modern ones, have Western-style dining rooms complete with table and chairs. Some wealthy people have both Western and Japanese dining rooms, as do many Japanese restaurants.

GARNISHES

Japanese food is nearly always charmingly garnished, with more variety and imagination than the ubiquitous parsley or lemon wedge. Some of the more frequently used garnishes are small translucent mounds of julienned carrot, cucumber or *daikon* (giant radish); crushed *nori* seaweed mixed with sesame seeds and salt, *furikake*, to sprinkle over rice or vegetables (see page 68); ghostly pale *enokitake* mushrooms that grow in delicate thread-like strands; tissue-thin, golden zucchini flowers; tiny green sprigs of watercress, young celery leaves or the beautiful *kinome* leaves; a twist or grating of lemon, lime or *yuzu* peel enhances most clear soups; a scattering of black or white sesame seeds, whichever provides the greater color contrast; shredded, paper thin seaweed; delicate green ovals of shredded spring onion; wafer-thin slices or strands of pink ginger or a fresh flower laid beside a dish. Plum blossoms are deftly cut from finely sliced carrots (plastic cutters are now available for the inexperienced) and look beautiful on small portions of salad or other vegetables or floated in soup. The following are a few easily made garnishes, but feel free to use your imagination with flowers or edible green sprigs to enhance the visual qualities of your Japanese meal and provide enlivening contrasts of taste and/or color.

Carrot Cherry Blossoms

1. Wash and trim the carrot. Cut out five wedges, lengthwise, at equal distances around the carrot.
2. Cut into slices and round off the edges to form rounded petals.
3. Leave as whole flowers or cut into individual petals which are arranged in flower shapes.

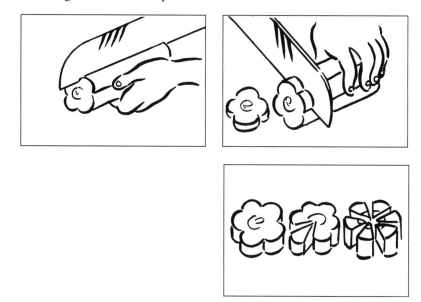

Tomato Rose

1. Submerge a large tomato in a bowl of boiling water for about a minute, then drain. With a very sharp knife, thinly pare off the skin in a spiral.
2. Wrap the skin around itself to form a flower. Two green bay leaves complete the effect.

Radish Waterlilies

1. Wash and trim the radishes. Make a ring of V-shaped cuts around the circumference.
2. Pull apart the two halves. Refrigerate in ice water for about an hour.

Fanned Radish

1. Wash and trim the radishes. Finely slice each radish without cutting right through to the base.
2. To open out the fan, refrigerate for about 2 hours in a bowl of ice water.

Needle-Cut Cucumber, Carrot, Giant Radish or Takuen Pickled Radish

Peel the carrot, cucumber or radish. With a very sharp knife cut the vegetables into very thin slices lengthwise, then slice across into very fine shreds. Serve heaped into small mounds.

Yuzu or Lemon Loops

1. Wash the fruit, cut into slices, then cut each slice in half. With a sharp knife cut between the rind and the flesh, stopping about 1-inch from the end.
2. Curl the peel around and under to form a loop.

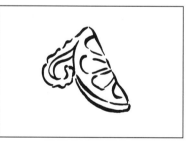

Spring Onion Tassels

1. Wash the spring onions. Cut off the bulb from one end and most of the green leaves from the other. With a very sharp knife, slice finely at either end of the trimmed onions.
2. To obtain a curled, tasseled effect, refrigerate in a bowl of ice water for about an hour.

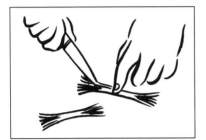 

Pine-Needle Twists

1. Cut out a small, rectangular piece of *takuen* pickled giant radish, or lemon, lime, *yuzu* or Seville orange peel. Trim into a neat, long rectangle. Make two cuts along the length of the rectangle, as shown.
2. Twist the two ends in opposite directions, so that one sits on the other.

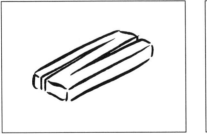 

CHOPSTICKS AND HOW TO USE THEM

Chopsticks, *hashi,* are the only implements used to eat an entire Japanese meal, with the exception of savory custard, *chawan mushi* (see page 136), which is eaten with a spoon. The chopsticks are made of washable, often beautifully inlaid and decorated lacquered wood, plain wood or bamboo. They are placed on the table in front of the diner, the thin ends resting on an ornamental chopstick rest and pointing to the left. Each member of the family has his or her own chopsticks which are washed after each meal and returned to their individual boxes. Guests are given a pair of disposable wooden chopsticks wrapped in a paper cover, *waribashi,* which remain joined at the thick end to show they have never been used. They are divided by the guest before eating and thrown away after the meal. Similar disposable chopsticks are provided when dining out. Several million pairs are used and thrown away every day in Japan. Most of the wood they are made of comes from the Malaysian rain forests, a practice that has decimated many areas of what used to be primeval forest. Some large companies, such as Mitsubishi, are now undertaking reforestation projects.

When not using your chopsticks during a meal it is good manners to replace them neatly on the chopstick rest, rather than resting them on bowls or plates. It is considered bad manners to use them to shovel food into your mouth from a bowl or dish, or to spear them through pieces of food. Never stick them into your rice to stand them up as this is a sign of death in Japan.

Chopsticks can soon be manipulated with confidence after a little practice, enabling you to pick up pieces of food neatly and with ease. They function rather like a pair of tongs, your thumb and first finger forming the hinge.

(1) Hold one chopstick lightly between your first two fingers and thumb, as though holding a pencil. This chopstick is moved up and down to take and hold pieces of food.

(2) Slide the second chopstick behind your thumb to rest between your second and third fingers. This chopstick is not moved up and down.

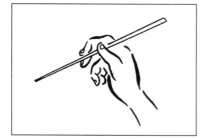 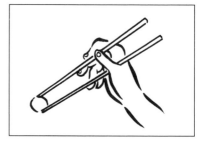

TAKING THE PLUNGE

The satisfaction of cooking a Japanese meal and the joy of eating it are impossible to describe. At your first attempt it is advisable not to cook too many dishes at the same time. A quick and easy Japanese meal, one that is very popular in Japan either for breakfast or as a snack or light meal, is a bowl of hot, thick, fermented soy bean paste, *miso*, soup (see page 35), containing a few vegetables and either some thin strips or chunky cubes of fried soy bean curd, *tofu*, served with a bowl of plain white rice, a few strips of *ajitsuke-nori* (seafood-flavored paper-thin seaweed to wrap round chunks of rice) and some crunchy pickled vegetables. Starting with a simple meal such as this, where you only need to cook one Japanese dish, will give you the feel of cooking and serving Japanese food, and the confidence to increase the number of dishes served at one meal. You will find a selection of suggested menus on pages 26–8.

Japanese vegetarian food has been called the "health" *cuisine* as well as the *haute cuisine* of vegetarian cooking and was the inspiration behind "*nouvelle cuisine.*" With the help of this book you will be able to produce delicious, healthy, authentic Japanese vegetarian snacks, dishes and menus in your own kitchen to delight yourself, your family and friends. Have fun, enjoy and "*bon appetit!*" or, as the Japanese would say, "*ita-dakimasu!*"

Huge snowflakes dance down.
Giant hailstones clatter
At the back door.
The dumplings are bubbling,
The red beans are boiling over,
The husband is returning,
The baby is screaming,
And I've lost the ladle.
What a life! What a life!

ANON (SEVENTEENTH CENTURY)

SUGGESTED MENUS

The luxury of eating a bowl of rice with every meal was a treat rarely enjoyed in the past by either the average urban Japanese or the rice farmer. Although over the centuries the rice-growing farmers were encouraged to produce ever greater quantities of rice, they were seldom allowed to keep enough of the precious grains to satisfactorily provide for themselves throughout the year. The Japanese saying that, out of ten, "six to the government, four to the people" or city dwellers illustrates what had long been their plight. Usually, other regional produce such as *daikon* radish (both root and leaves), millet, barley or sweet potatoes would be mixed with a very little rice and either steamed, *katemeshi,* or boiled into a sort of broth, *zosui.* In a few areas, grains, noodles or sweet potatoes were staples, and rice was often not eaten at all. During the period of rationing that followed the Second World War, rice was evenly distributed to every part of Japan and became the main staple for the whole country.

Even when it was possible for ordinary Japanese to eat a bowl of rice with every main meal, this meal was known as, until quite recently, *Ichiju Issai,* "one soup, one dish," which illustrates the frugality that so often attended the mealtime scene for most Japanese families. The soup was usually fermented soy bean paste, *miso,* soup; the "dish," or *okazu,* would be either a small portion of some sort of protein, or either fresh or pickled vegetable. Rice would always accompany the "one soup, one dish." This modest meal was traditionally eaten from an individual square, often lacquered box, *hazoken,* which contained one soup bowl, one rice bowl, one small dish and a pair of chopsticks. It was only on festive occasions that, until quite recently, the ordinary Japanese person could enjoy as many as three, or if they were lucky up to five, *okazu*, or side dishes accompanied by soup, rice and pickles.

In contrast, the meals of the aristocracy and richer families could contain up to 14 or 15 different *okazu* dishes cooked in a variety of ways such as fried, simmered or vinegared. In addition a savory custard, *chawan mushi*, could also be served as well as both clear and *miso* soup, rice and pickles.

A repast of similarly grand dimensions enjoyed today is the *kaiseki* or "gathering together" meal which had its origins in the Japanese tea ceremony. Nowadays it is primarily eaten in quality restaurants. Companies often entertain valued business clients by treating them to this most impressive and extremely expensive meal, which can cost hundreds of dollars per head. But the expense is worth it—the liberally flowing *sake* often oils the wheels of many a lucrative business deal.

With the increasing prosperity of the average Japanese, the "one soup, one dish" has given way to an everyday family main meal consisting of two or three different vegetable and protein *okazu* dishes plus soup, rice and pickles. The celebratory meals enjoyed by most Japanese today, such as coming of age parties, funerals and traditional Japanese wedding receptions, call for a greater number of *okazu* dishes and can consist of unusual and costly ingredients prepared with time-consuming specialized skills. Fresh fruits can conclude the meal. If the host wishes to impress his guests, out-of-season fruits will definitely make an impression.

Although noodles and Japanese pizza, *okonomi yaki*, do not normally form part of the main meal of the day, we occasionally enjoy them as part of our evening meal. Apart from these, and one-pot casseroles and snacks, most of the vegetable and protein dishes in this book are the *okazu* or dishes that form part of a meal consisting of several small dishes rather than being, as is so often in the West, the one vegetable or single main dish served with the carbohydrate such as potatoes or pasta.

Here are a few suggestions to show you how simple it is to prepare a Japanese snack or light meal, and how easily you can put together a balanced main meal by selecting a soup, a *tofu* and/or egg dish, vegetables and/or salad, rice and pickles. Do try to include both soft and crisp foods in the same meal.

Unless specifically stated, garnishes have not been included in the recipes—please read the section on garnishes on pages 16-20. Also "What to Drink with a Japanese Meal" is helpful, see page 12.

Light Meals, Lunches or Snacks

Fried Noodles with Vegetables, Yakisoba, PAGE 81
Fried Egg with Powdered Seaweed

▪

Japanese-style Vegetable Spring Rolls, Harumaki, PAGE 126
Salad
Rice or Noodles (optional)

▪

Vegetable Pancake, Okonomi Yaki, PAGE 118
Salad and/or Soup

▪

Soy Bean Paste Soup with Chunky Fried Bean Curd and Sweet Potatoes, Atsuage To Satsumaimo No Misoshiru, PAGE 42
Rice
Pickles

▪

Twenty-minute meal—Ramen Noodles with Fried Soy Bean Curd and Broccoli, Chan Pon Men, PAGE 82

▪

Seaweed Cornets Stuffed with Sushi Rice, Temaki, PAGE 66
Salad
Condiments—Japanese horseradish paste (wasabi), or sweet pickled ginger (shoga-ama-zuke), soy sauce
Soup or iced Japanese beer

▪

Thick or Thin Sushi Rolls, Futomaki or Hosomaki, PAGES 64 AND 62
Salad
Condiments—Japanese horseradish paste (wasabi), soy sauce
Soup or iced Japanese beer

▪

Main Meals

Crisp-coated Deep-fried Tofu, Agedashi Dofu, PAGE 85
Spring Rain Noodles and Cucumber Salad, Harusame To Kyurino
Sunomono, PAGE 145
Spinach Rolls with Sesame Seeds, Horenso No Ohitashi, PAGE 116
Egg Drop Soup with Snow Peas, Kakitama Jiru, PAGE 37
Rice
Pickles
■

Chilled Silken Tofu, Hya Yakko, PAGE 86
Chilled Buckwheat Noodles, Zaru Soba, PAGE 80
A few pieces of Deep-fried Vegetables in a Light Crispy Batter,
Yasai No Tempura, PAGE 119
Chilled Giant Radish and Carrot Salad, Daikon Namasu, PAGE 140
Clear Soup with Cucumber and Watercress, Kyuri No Suimono, PAGE 32
■

Gingered Fried Tofu, Shoga Yaki Dofu, PAGE 91
Rolled Onion Omelet, Negi Tamago Yaki, PAGE 134
Sautéed Cucumber and Mushrooms,
Kuri To Shiitake No Toroni, PAGE 106
Lotus Root and Sweet Red Pepper Salad in Sake Dressing,
Renkon Ae, PAGE 142
Soy Bean Paste Soup with Bean Curd Strips and Spring Onions,
Aburage To Negi No Misoshiru, PAGE 41
Rice
Pickles
■

Braised Deep-fried Tofu with Leeks, Niranegi To Yaki Dofu, PAGE 90
Seaweed Egg Rolls, Nori Tamago Yaki, PAGE 131
Broccoli with Sesame Seeds, Burokkori No Goma Shoyu Kake, PAGE 114
Sautéed Lotus Root, Renkon Kimpira, PAGE 108
Clear Soup with Fresh Bean Curd and Spring Onion,
Tofu Negi No Suimono, PAGE 31
Rice
Pickles
■

Ganmodoki and Vegetables in Sweet Vinegar Sauce,
Ganmodoki To Yasai No Itame-Ni, PAGE 94
Japanese Squash Simmered in Rice Wine and Soy Sauce,
Kabocha No Toroni, PAGE 112
Fried Soy Bean Curd Rolls Stuffed with Fresh Tofu and Vegetables,
Inari Maki, PAGE 88
Bean Sprout and Cucumber Salad with Japanese Horseradish Dressing,
Moyashino Wasabi Ae, PAGE 139
Rice
Pickles
Soup
▨

Fried Noodles with Vegetables, Yakisoba, PAGE 81
Golden Patties of Fresh Tofu and Vegetables, Ganmodoki, PAGE 92
Seaweed and Cucumber Salad, Kyuri No Wakame Ae, PAGE 138
Soup
▨

Braised Golden Patties of Fresh Tofu, Ganmodoki Itame-Ni, PAGE 93
Lotus Root and Sweet Red Pepper Salad in Sake Dressing,
Renkon Ae, *page 142*
Rice Wine and Sesame-Fried Carrots, Ninjin No Shoyu Age, PAGE 117
Spinach Rolls with Sesame Seeds, Horenso No Ohitashi, PAGE 116
Two Seaweed Soup, Wakame No Misoshiru, PAGE 43
Rice
Pickles
▨

Deep-fried Vegetables in a Light Crispy Batter, Yasai No Tempura
PAGE 119
Crisp-coated Deep-fried Tofu, Agedashi Dofu, PAGE 85
Soup
Rice
Pickles
▨

Rice Balls and Triangles, Onigiri, PAGE 47
Stuffed Soy Bean Curd, Inari Zushi, PAGE 61
Sautéed Lotus Root, Renkon Kimpira, PAGE 108
Cucumber and Watercress Salad in Pickled Plum Dressing,
Kyuri No Umeboshi Ae, PAGE 143
Soup or Japanese Green Tea, PAGE 153
Condiments—Japanese Horseradish Paste (wasabi), *soy sauce*
▨

JAPANESE SOUP

For soup
To begin,
Tasty Suizenji seaweed.

BASHO (1644-1694)

Soup is a must at most Japanese meals including break-fast, and is taken throughout the meal rather than as a separate course. It is served in deep, lidded bowls designed to retain the heat throughout the meal. There are two basic types of Japanese soup, miso shiru *(thick), and* sui-mono *(clear). Both are simple to make and provide a deli-cious and elegant accompaniment to your Japanese meal.*

CLEAR SOUP
■ S U I M O N O ■

A bowl of clear Japanese soup should be, ideally, as exquisite to behold as it is delicious to taste. Clear soups are served partly to refresh and clear the mouth during a meal, and are com-posed of a delicately flavored stock, *dashi*, into which are immersed various combinations of tasty morsels according to their seasonal availability.

There are several types of *dashi* used in Japanese cooking. The very delicate, seafood flavored *kombu-dashi* is made simply by soaking approximately 5 inches of *kombu* (kelp seaweed) in about 4 cups of water for an hour. It is brought slowly to a boil and the seaweed is then removed. The fragrant *shiitake-dashi* is simply water in which dried *shiitake* mushrooms have been soaked. A very simple, refreshing, vegetarian clear soup may be made using either

the *shiitake* or *kombu dashi* as a base, while the following vegetarian *dashi* recipe makes a more richly flavorful and aromatic soup
base. It is also excellent when *dashi* is called for in a recipe.

A fragrant garnish of, say, a twist of lemon peel, a piquant green
sprig, a scattering of toasted sesame seeds, some shredded spring
onion or a squeeze of ginger completes your chosen clear soup.

DASHI
▪ VEGETARIAN STOCK ▪

SERVES 4

Makes approximately
2 1/2 cups clear soup stock
sufficient for 4 bowls of soup

SEAWEEDS TASTE of the sea, as do fish, and the two seaweeds in this vegetarian *dashi* recipe impart their delicate seafood flavor, without the
need to add fish or dried tuna flakes, *bonito*, which are found in many
traditional *dashis*. Vegetarian *dashi* is used in the exquisite soups and
dishes served in some traditional Buddhist temples. It should be nice
and clear with a clean, unobtrusive flavor and pleasing, fresh aroma.

Dashi is also used as a stock in Japanese cooking. It is no more difficult to make than homemade Western stocks. If you are going to
cook Japanese food regularly, it's a good idea to make more than is
required and freeze the surplus. Instant *dashi* stock cubes or powder,
which are used in the same way as Western stock cubes, are very convenient and can be bought from Japanese food shops in this country, but most of them contain fish.

4 cups cold water
5-inch piece
  of *kombu* (kelp) seaweed
3 dried *shiitake* mushrooms
1/2 ounce *tororo-kombu* seaweed
2 tablespoons *sake* (fortified rice wine)

2 teaspoons *mirin*
  (sweet rice wine)
1/2 teaspoon sugar
2 1/2 tablespoons Japanese
  soy sauce

DO NOT wash *kombu,* the powdery patches contain much of the flavor. Dust off any sand with a dry cloth. With scissors, cut the *kombu* three-quarters of the way through in three or four different places.

■ Put the water, *kombu* and *shiitake* mushrooms in a saucepan and soak for 3–4 hours. A small plate on the mushrooms will keep them submerged. Remove plate and bring to just below a boil very slowly. Remove *kombu* just below boiling point.

■ Add *tororo-kombu* to the *shiitake* mushrooms and bring to a boil. Simmer for 5 minutes.

■ Add remaining ingredients. Return to a boil and simmer for 2 minutes. Drain well through a colander or sieve.

TOFU NEGI NO SUIMONO
■ CLEAR SOUP WITH FRESH BEAN CURD AND SPRING ONION ■

SERVES 4

I FIRST had this simple and elegant soup at the Ra-ra Japanese restaurant in Kathmandu, which was run by two young expatriate Japanese. This is the variety of soup most often served with a meal at a Japanese restaurant. Use silken *tofu* rather than ordinary or cotton *tofu* (see pages 161-2).

■
1 block of silken *tofu* (about 10 1/2 ounces)
2 spring onions
■

■
3 1/2 *dashi* (see page 30)
toasted sesame seeds
■

REMEMBER SILKEN *tofu* is very fragile. Carefully place *tofu* on a plate and cut into 8 equal-sized cubes.

■ Trim the roots and any damaged leaves from the spring onions. Wash well and finely shred diagonally.

■ Put *dashi* in a saucepan. Gently lower the *tofu* pieces into the *dashi* and bring to a boil. Simmer for about 1 minute. Carefully remove *tofu,* placing 2 pieces into each of 4 soup bowls. Sprinkle over a few sesame seeds and the spring onions. Carefully pour over a hot *dashi* and serve immediately.

KYURI NO SUIMONO
■ CLEAR SOUP WITH CUCUMBER AND WATERCRESS ■

SERVES 4

THIS DELIGHTFUL soup is most refreshing on a hot day—the flavors of summer flecked with fragrant lemon peel.

■

1/2 cucumber
salad mustard and watercress
3 1/2 cups *dashi* (see page 30)

■

■

grated peel of 1 *yuzu*, lemon or
  Seville orange

■

PEEL THE cucumber and cut in half lengthwise. Remove the seeds with a teaspoon and cut into paper-thin slices. Put in a colander and set aside.

■ Wash watercress. Remove seed husks, if any, and shake dry.

■ Put *dashi* into a saucepan and bring to a boil.

■ Pour a kettle of boiling water through the cucumber slices to warm them. Drain and arrange in the bottom of 4 soup bowls. Sprinkle over the grated citrus peel and pour over a boiling *dashi*. Garnish with the watercress and serve immediately.

SHIITAKE TO WAKAME NO SUIMONO

■ CLEAR SOUP WITH FRESH *SHIITAKE* MUSHROOM AND *WAKAME* SEAWEED ■

SERVES 4

SUCCULENT PIECES of mushroom and tasty seaweed combine to make a delicious soup.

■

1 length or 5 gram packet of
  dried *wakame* seaweed
2 spring onions

■

■

4 fresh *shiitake*, or medium-cap
  mushrooms
3 1/2 cups *dashi* (see page 30)

■

SOAK THE packet of *wakame* in warm water for 20 minutes, or until expanded and soft, then drain. If using length of wakame, soak as above, remove the hard edge and discard, then cut remaining length of *wakame* into 1/2-inch bite-sized pieces.

■ Trim the roots and any damaged leaves from the spring onions. Wash well and finely shred diagonally.

■ Wash the mushrooms, remove any tough stalks and slice each mushroom into 3 or 4 slices.

■ Bring *dashi* to a boil. Add mushrooms and simmer for 2-3 minutes until tender. Add *wakame* and simmer for the last minute. Ladle into 4 bowls and sprinkle over the spring onions. Serve immediately.

UZURA NO TAMAGO TO HORENSO NO SUIMONO

■ CLEAR SOUP WITH QUAIL'S EGG AND SPINACH ■

SERVES 4

TINY, BEAUTIFULLY flecked and spotted quails' eggs are very common in Japan, and are sold in boxes of twelve. They add a touch of luxury to clear soup for a special meal.

■
6 ounces fresh spinach
4 fresh quails' eggs
■

■
3 1/2 cups *dashi* (see page 30)
4 slivers of lemon peel
■

BOIL THE quails' eggs for 2 minutes. Remove shells and set aside.
■ Remove tough stems from spinach and wash well. Cut into 1-inch lengths.
■ Bring *dashi* to a boil. Add spinach and simmer for 1-2 minutes. Ladle the spinach soup into 4 soup bowls. Top with a quail's egg and sliver of lemon peel. Serve immediately.

TOFU DANGO TO NEGI NO SUIMONO

■ CLEAR SOUP WITH *TOFU* DUMPLINGS AND SIMMERED LEEKS ■

SERVES 4

THESE DELICATE light dumplings are very easy to make and are always a favorite in winter soups. Serve this soup with a meal, or crack an egg into the soup to poach in the hot liquid and serve with plain white rice and some crunchy Japanese pickles for a delicious and nourishing light meal.

about 10 ounces fresh tofu
2 leeks
2 eggs
2 tablespoons flour

2 teaspoons *mirin*
  (sweet rice wine)
1 teaspoon salt
3 1/2 cups *dashi* (see page 30)

WRAP THE *tofu* in a clean kitchen towel and leave for 30 minutes to remove excess water.

■ Trim the roots and any tough leaves from the leeks. Wash well and cut into 1/4-inch lengths.

■ Mash *tofu* into a smooth paste. Add eggs, flour, *mirin* and salt and thoroughly blend.

■ Put *dashi* and leeks into a saucepan and bring to a boil.

■ Divide the *tofu* mixture into 8 portions and form each portion into a ball. Lower the *tofu* dumplings carefully into a boiling *dashi*. Bring back to a boil and simmer gently for 5 minutes, or until the dumplings float to the surface and the leeks are tender.

■ Remove dumplings very carefully from the soup and put 2 into each of 4 soup bowls. Pour over the leek soup and serve immediately.

Five dumplings
Wrapped in bamboo leaves—
No message, no name.

RANSETSU (1654-1707)

TAKENOKO TO WAKAME NO SUIMONO
■ CLEAR SOUP WITH BAMBOO SHOOT AND *WAKAME* SEAWEED ■

SERVES 4

BAMBOO GROWS taller, faster than any other living thing, and some varieties have been measured as growing almost 4 feet in 24 hours. In Japan their tender, fresh young shoots are a symbol of spring, when their crispness and flavor are at their best. Canned bamboo shoots are a rather poor substitute and are not suitable for this dish.

■
1 length or 5-gram packet of dried
   wakame seaweed
about 8 ounces fresh bamboo shoots
■

■
1 3/4 cups *dashi* (see page 30)
■

SOAK THE sachet of *wakame* in warm water for 20 minutes, or until expanded and soft, then drain. If using length of *wakame*, soak as above, remove the hard edge and discard, then cut remaining length of *wakame* into bite-sized pieces about 1/2-inch long.

■ Wash bamboo shoots well, cover with lightly salted cold water and bring to a boil. Simmer for about 30 minutes, or until tender. Drain and remove skin. Cut into thin slices about l/2-inch wide by 1 1/2-inches long.

■ Bring *dashi* to a boil. Add bamboo shoots and *wakame*, return to a boil and simmer for 1 minute. Ladle into four soup bowls and serve immediately.

KAKITAMA JIRU
■ EGG DROP SOUP WITH SNOW PEAS ■

SERVES 4

Egg drop or "thread" soup appears in many Far Eastern cuisines. This Japanese version combines soft, succulent egg and crispy snow peas for a special soup of enticing textures and flavors.

16 fresh snow peas
3 eggs

3 1/2 cups *dashi* (see page 30)

WASH AND trim the snow peas. Cut in half diagonally. Boil very briefly in slightly salted water until just cooked but still crisp (*al dente*). Drain and reserve.

■ Bring *dashi* to a boil.

■ Beat eggs thoroughly.

■ Stir a boiling *dashi* until it forms a slow whirlpool. Pour in the beaten eggs in a thin stream, while at the same time drawing up the resulting partly cooked egg strands with a fork or chopsticks, so that it separates into small pieces.

■ Ladle into 4 soup bowls and arrange the snow peas on top. Serve immediately.

KINOKO TO MOCHI NO SUIMONO
■ CLEAR SOUP WITH SHIITAKE MUSHROOMS AND STICKY RICE CAKE ■

SERVES 4

STICKY RICE cakes, mochi (see page 54-5), are thought to promote strength and stamina. Combining them in a clear soup with succulent mushrooms and a dash of spicy pepper produces delicious contrasts of flavors and textures.

■

4 fresh *shiitake* or medium cap
   mushrooms
3 1/2 cups *dashi* (see page 30)

■

4 *mochi* (sticky rice cakes)
vegetable oil for frying, optional
schichimi-togarashi (Japanese
   seven-spice pepper)

■

■

WASH THE mushrooms, remove any tough stalks and slice each mushroom into 3 or 4 slices.

■ Bring *dashi* to a boil, add mushrooms and simmer for 2-3 minutes.

■ Grill the *mochi* or fry for a few minutes in a little vegetable oil over a medium heat, turning once, until puffed up and golden brown.

■ Put 1 *mochi* in the bottom of each of 4 soup bowls. Ladle over the mushroom soup. Sprinkle a pinch of *schichimi-togarashi* and serve immediately.

TAMAGO YAKI TO SERI NO SUIMONO
■ CLEAR SOUP WITH EGG STRIPS AND WATERCRESS ■

SERVES 4

The green, peppery crispness of watercress and succulent, golden ribbons of egg attractively combine in a refreshing and nourishing soup.

2 eggs
1 teaspoon Japanese soy sauce
vegetable oil

1 bunch of watercress
3 1/2 cups *dashi* (see page 30)
toasted sesame seeds

BEAT THE eggs with soy sauce.

Lightly oil a frying pan. Pour in the eggs and make an omelet, turning once. Remove carefully and lay on absorbent paper towels. Pat excess oil off the top with a sheet of paper towels. Using scissors or a sharp knife, cut into long, thin strips about 1/4-inch wide and set aside.

■ Cut off the green sprigs and leaves from the watercress, discarding coarse stems and any fading or damaged leaves. Wash well, then coarsely chop.

■ Bring *dashi* to a boil and add watercress. Return to a boil and simmer for 1 minute.

■ Arrange egg strips in the bottom of 4 soup bowls. Pour over a boiling watercress soup and sprinkle over a few sesame seeds.

THICK SOUPS
▪ S H I R U   M O N O ▪

Thick Japanese soups are usually made with fermented soy bean paste, *miso*, which according to Japanese mythology was a gift from the gods. It has a rich taste and aroma and is a valuable food source, being high in protein, minerals, essential amino acids and the B vitamins, including B^{12}. It is also low in calories and fat.

There are basically four types of *miso*: *shiru miso* is white and sweet; *inaka miso* is a golden color; *aka miso* or red *miso* is a reddish-chestnut color with a heavier flavor; and *sendai miso* is also a reddish chestnut color with a heavier salt content. Each of these four basic types of *miso* varies a lot from one producer to another, and which to use in your soup is mostly a matter of personal taste. I prefer a golden-colored *inaka miso* which states on the package that it is low in salt. It has a good rounded flavor without being too salty.

There are not really very many varieties of *miso* soup. They are basically a few vegetables cooked in a *dashi* stock into which a little *miso* paste is stirred, with maybe some added *tofu*. The following recipes are typical, but any vegetables in any combination can be used, such as shredded Chinese cabbage, broccoli florets, carrot matchsticks, bean sprouts, potatoes, sliced leeks—so feel free to experiment.

Although *miso* soup is very quick and easy to make, instant *miso* soups are even quicker. They are of surprisingly good quality and come in packages of various delicious varieties. Each package contains several small individual packets which you just tip into your soup bowl, pour over boiling water and stir. Seaweeds, vegetables, small pieces of *tofu* and garnishes, according to the variety, appear like magic in a rich and tasty *miso* soup. They complement any Japanese meal and are worth using occasionally, not only because of their superlative quality compared to most instant soups, but because they also help save time and hassle if you are preparing several other Japanese dishes, or if you would like to have soup with a quickly prepared Japanese snack.

ABURAGE TO NEGI NO MISOSHIRU
■ SOY BEAN PASTE SOUP WITH BEAN CURD STRIPS AND SPRING ONIONS ■

■ SERVES 4

THIS IS the simple and classic way to prepare *miso* soup. It is richly flavored and very high in protein.

4 pieces of *aburage* (flat sheets of fried soy bean curd)
8 spring onions

1/2 water and 1/2 *dashi* (see page 30) totalling 3 1/2 cups liquid
6 tablespoons *inska miso* (golden *miso* paste)

PUT *ABURAGE* in a bowl and pour over boiling water to remove excess oil. Drain and cut into strips, widthwise, about 1/2-inch wide.

■ Trim roots and any damaged parts from spring onions and wash well. Shred 2 spring onions very finely on the diagonal and cut the remaining spring onions into 1-inch lengths.

■ Put water and *dashi* mixture into a saucepan. Add *aburage* and bring to a boil. Add the 1-inch pieces spring onions and simmer for 1 minute. Mix the *miso* paste into a smooth cream with some of the hot *dashi*/water and stir it into the soup. Return to just below boiling point.

■ Ladle into 4 soup bowls, sprinkle over shredded spring onions and serve immediately.

ATSUAGE TO SATSUMAIMO NO MISOSHIRU
▪ SOY BEAN PASTE SOUP WITH CHUNKY FRIED BEAN CURD AND SWEET POTATOES ▪

SERVES 4

A TYPICAL country soup, hearty, rich and satisfying on a cold winter's day. Very high in protein and a meal in itself served with plain white rice and Japanese pickles.

▪

about 10 ounces fresh *tofu*
1 sweet or Irish potato
3 spring onions
2 carrots
vegetable oil for deep-frying

▪

1/2 water and 1/2 *dashi* (see page 30) totaling
1 3/4 pints liquid
6 tablespoons *inaka miso* (golden *miso* paste)

▪

WRAP TOFU in a clean kitchen towel and leave for about 20 minutes to remove excess water. Cut into twelve equal sized cubes.

▪ Peel sweet potato and cut into bite-sized cubes.

▪ Remove roots and any damaged leaves from spring onions. Wash well and shred very finely, diagonally.

▪ Peel carrots and cut into matchsticks.

▪ Heat oil to 350°F and deep-fry *tofu* until crisp and golden on the outside. Drain on absorbent paper towels.

▪ Put water and *dashi* mixture into a saucepan and bring to a boil. Add sweet potato, carrots and *tofu*. Simmer until the vegetables are just done.

▪ Mix the *miso* paste into a smooth cream with some of the hot *dashi*/water mixture and stir it into the soup. Bring back to just below boiling point.

▪ Ladle the soup into 4 soup bowls and sprinkle over the shredded spring onions. Serve immediately.

Seaweed
Caught between rocks
Forgotten tides.

KITO (1740-1787)

WAKAME NO MISOSHIRU
■TWO SEAWEED SOUP■

SERVES 4

A SIMPLY prepared, extremely tasty soup combining the subtle seafood flavors of the seaweeds and the richness of *miso*.

two 5-gram packets of dried
   wakame seaweed
4 spring onions
4 packets of *ajitsuke-nori* seaweed
1/2 water and 1/2 *dashi* (see page
   30) totalling 3 1/2 cups liquid

6 1/2 tablespoons *inaka miso*
   (golden *miso* paste)
about 16-20 *fu* (small pieces of
   dried gluten), optional

SOAK THE packets of *wakame* seaweed in warm water for 20 minutes, or until expanded and soft, then drain. If using lengths of *wakame*, soak as above, remove the hard edge and discard, then cut remaining length of *wakame* into 1/2-inch bite-sized pieces.

■ Trim roots and any damaged parts from spring onions and wash well. Shred finely, diagonally.

■ Cut *ajitsuke-nori* seaweed into fine strips, lengthwise.

■ Put the water and *dashi* mixture into a saucepan. Add *wakame* seaweed. Bring to a boil and simmer for 1 minute.

■ Mix the *miso* paste into a smooth cream with some of the hot *dashi*/water and stir it into the soup. Add the *fu* and bring back to just below boiling point.

■ Ladle the soup into 4 bowls. Sprinkle over the spring onions and strips of *ajitsuke-nori* seaweed. Serve immediately.

RICE AND RICE DISHES

■ G O H A N   M O N O ■

There's rice in my bag
For ten days,
And a bundle of firewood
By the hearth.

RYOKAN (1757-1831)

Unlike the ideal of "every grain separate" in the West, perfectly cooked Japanese rice is tender, moist, glossy and slightly glutinous, so that the grains cling together, making it easy to pick up a portion with chopsticks.

Until quite recently, rice was traditionally cooked in a lidded pot or saucepan. Nowadays, almost all Japanese housewives and restaurants have electric rice cookers. They are so easy to use; you just put in the rice and water and switch on. It automatically boils, steams and keeps the perfectly cooked rice warm until you need it. Rice cookers can be bought in Japanese and Chinese food shops in this country and if you cook rice on a regular basis, it is well worth investing in one. I was given a rice cooker in Japan and it was wonderful to come home in the evening to perfectly cooked, hot rice.

A lot of rice is now imported in Japan from America where it is grown in dry fields, unlike the flooded paddy fields of Japan. As Japan exports hardly any rice, American-Japanese rice, which is almost identical, is sold in Japanese food shops in this country. Although not quite as authentic, other rices such as

Chinese or Indian may be eaten with a Japanese meal. Please note, however, that if Japanese rice is stipulated in a recipe then Japanese or American-Japanese rice must be used to obtain the required result.

The following recipe is the traditional way of cooking Japanese rice. It is difficult to give the exact amount of water required as the water content of rice decreases with age, and varies with the type of rice used, the location it was grown in, and the way it was grown. However a rough rule of thumb is five parts of rice to six parts of water. With a little practice you will be able to find the correct proportions for the type of rice you buy.

GOHAN
■ PLAIN RICE ■

SERVES 4

THIS IS the fragrant, delicately flavored glossy white rice most often served with a Japanese meal. Salt is never added to Japanese plain white rice—saltiness is obtained by eating the rice with a salty Japanese pickle.

1 3/4 cups Japanese rice

about 2 1/4 cups water

PUT THE rice in a large heavy-bottomed saucepan. Place it in the sink under a running cold tap. Stir the rice carefully in the water with your hand or a wire whisk while allowing the water (but not the rice) to overflow. Continue until the water becomes almost clean.

■ Drain the rice in a sieve or colander and return to the saucepan. Add the water and leave to soak for 1 hour, during which time the rice will absorb some water, partially softening the grains.

■ Cover with a tight lid. Do not lift the lid throughout the cooking and final steaming process. Turn the heat to its highest and bring very quickly to a boil. Steam will appear around the edge of the lid when boiling point is reached. Reduce the heat and simmer very gently for 15 minutes. Turn the heat up to its highest for 10 seconds. Turn off the heat and leave the rice to stand on the stove for 10 minutes to finish cooking by steaming in its own heat.

■ Dampen a bamboo rice paddle or wooden spatula and gently cut into the rice to release some steam before serving. If not serving immediately, place a clean kitchen towel over the saucepan before replacing the lid to absorb the steam and keep the rice fluffy.

■ Serve hot in small individual bowls, as it is or sprinkled with *furikake*, seasoning garnish for rice (see pages 68-9).

Glaring gloomily at the sky,
Pecking at their picnic boxes
At home.

ANON

ONIGIRI
■ RICE BALLS AND TRIANGLES ■

SERVES 4

ONIGIRI ARE a very tasty and visually attractive way to serve rice. They are usually included in lunch and picnic boxes and are also popular as snacks or as part of a cold buffet.

■

4 *umeboshi* (pickled plums) or
 umeboshi paste
1 1/2-inch piece of *takuan*
 (pickled giant radish)
3 1/2 tablespoons toasted black
 sesame seeds

■

salt
hot, cooked plain rice made with
 1 3/4 Japanese rice
 (see page 46)
2 packets *ajitsuke-nori* seaweed
shoga-ama-zuke (pickled ginger)

■

REMOVE THE stones from the *umeboshi*

■ Grate the *takuan* pickle on a coarse cheese grater and drain on absorbent paper towels.

■ Put the sesame seeds on a plate and sprinkle some salt on another plate. Put some lightly salted water into a bowl.

■ Divide the hot rice into three equal portions:

■ **Portion one** Divide the rice again into 4 portions. Dampen your palms lightly with the salted water and press each palm onto the salted plate to dust very lightly with salt. Pick up a portion of rice and roll firmly into a ball without squashing the grains of rice. Roll the rice ball into the sesame seeds to coat. Repeat with the remaining three portions of rice.

■ **Portion two** Divide the rice again into four equal portions and roll into rice balls as before, but do not coat in sesame seeds. Press your little finger into the center of each rice ball. Insert an *umeboshi* or 1/4 teaspoon of *umeboshi* paste and smooth over the hole to close it. Flatten the rice balls to make a sort of patty, then shape into thick, sturdy triangles that can stand up. Place one strip of *ajitsuke-nori* seaweed across the peak of each triangle and press down so it adheres to the two straight edges. Place another strip across each base, pressing until it adheres.

■ **Portion three** Divide the rice again into 4 equal portions and proceed as portion two, substituting shredded *takuan* pickle for the *umeboshi*.

■ Place one piece of each variety of *onigiri* onto 4 small dishes. Garnish with a little ginger pickle and serve. If not serving immediately, cover with a clean cloth and eat within a few hours.

SEKIHAN
■ STICKY RED RICE ■

SERVES 4

RED IS a festive color in Japan, and red rice has been eaten for centuries on special festive occasions. Sticky red rice is made with a glutinous white rice, *mochi-gome*, and red *adzuki* beans, known in Japan as the king of beans.

■

2/3 cup red *adzuki* beans
2 1/2 cups *mochi gome*
  (glutinous rice)

■

■

1 1/2 teaspoons salt
1 tablespoon black toasted
  sesame seeds

■

SOAK THE *adzuki* beans overnight in plenty of cold water. Drain and wash well under running water. Put the beans in a large saucepan with plenty of cold water, bring to a boil, then simmer for about 1 hour, or until the beans are soft but still granular in texture, adding more boiling water if necessary. Do not allow the beans to become mushy. Drain the beans, reserving the cooking water. Cover the beans to prevent them drying out.

■ Put rice into a deep, heavy-bottomed saucepan. Put the saucepan in the sink under a running cold tap, and stir gently with your hands or a wire whisk for a few minutes, while allowing the water to overflow until it becomes almost clear. Drain the rice in a colander or sieve. Put the rice into a large, lidded saucepan. Add enough cold water to the reserved cooled cooking water, if necessary, to make it up to 2 1/2 cups and add to the rice. Leave to soak for 1 hour during which time the rice will absorb some water, partially softening the grains.

■ Add the beans and salt to the rice and stir gently. Cover with a tight lid. Do not lift the lid during the remaining cooking and final steaming process. Bring to a boil. Steam will appear around the edge of the lid when boiling point is reached. Reduce heat and simmer gently for 15 minutes. Raise the heat to maximum possible and cook for a further 10 seconds. Turn off the heat and leave the rice on the stove to steam in its own heat for 15 minutes.

■ Dampen a bamboo rice paddle or wooden spatula and gently cut into the rice to release some steam, while carefully turning over to distribute the *adzuki* beans. Serve hot in small individual bowls with a few toasted sesame seeds sprinkled over the top.

■ If not serving immediately, place a kitchen towel over the pan before replacing the lid, to absorb the steam and keep the rice fluffy.

Storm —
Chestnuts racing across
The bamboo porch.

SHIKI (1867-1902)

KURI GOHAN
■ CHESTNUT RICE ■

SERVES 4

A FAVORITE autumn rice when the juicy, crisp chestnuts are freshly harvested. The Italian chestnuts available here are slightly larger than Japanese ones but are otherwise identical. The chestnuts remain a little crisp to contrast with the soft rice.

20 fresh chestnuts	2 tablespoons *sake*
1 3/4 cup Japanese rice	1 1/2 teaspoons salt
2 1/4 cups water	

SOAK THE chestnuts overnight in plenty of water to plump them up a little and loosen the skin. Drain and remove outer shell and inner skin. Cut chestnuts in half and set aside.

■ Put the rice in a deep pan. Place it under a running cold tap. Stir the rice carefully in the water with your hand or a wire whisk allowing the water to overflow until it becomes almost clear.

■ Drain the rice in a colander or sieve, add 2 1/4 cups water and leave to soak for 1 hour during which time the rice will have absorbed some of the water, partially softening the grains.

■ Add the chestnuts, *sake*, and salt and stir gently. Cover with a tight lid. Do not lift the lid throughout the remaining cooking and steaming process. Bring quickly to a boil over a high heat. Steam will appear around the edge of the lid when boiling point is reached. Reduce the heat and simmer very gently for 15 minutes. Turn up the heat to maximum for 10 seconds, then turn off and leave the rice on the stove to steam in its own heat for 10 minutes.

■ Dampen a bamboo rice paddle or wooden spatula and gently turn over the rice to release some steam and distribute the chestnuts. If not serving immediately, place a clean kitchen towel over the saucepan before replacing the lid to absorb the steam and keep the rice fluffy. Serve hot in small individual bowls.

MIDORI PEA GOHAN
■ GREEN PEA RICE ■

SERVES 4

A SURPRISINGLY delicious rice to serve with any meal. Leftover rice can be given a lift by adding spring onions and peas and heating it up in the microwave.

■

8 spring onions
1 3/4 cups Japanese rice
2 1/4 cups water

■

1 1/2 teaspoons salt
1 cup lightly cooked fresh
   or frozen green peas

TRIM THE roots and any damaged parts from the spring onions and wash well. Shred finely diagonally and set aside.

■ Put the rice in a deep saucepan. Place it in the sink under a running cold tap. Stir the rice carefully with your hand or a wire whisk while allowing the water to overflow until it becomes almost clear. Drain rice in a colander or sieve and return to the saucepan. Add 2 1/4 cups water and leave to soak for 1 hour, during which time the rice will absorb some of the water, partially softening the grains.

■ Add salt and stir gently. Cover with a tight lid. Do not remove the lid throughout the remaining cooking and final steaming process. Bring very quickly to a boil over a high heat. Steam will appear around the edge of the lid when boiling point is reached. Reduce the heat and simmer very gently for 15 minutes. Turn up the heat to its highest for 10 seconds, then turn off the heat and leave the rice to stand on the stove to steam in its own heat for 10 minutes.

■ Add peas and spring onions to the rice. Dampen a bamboo rice paddle or wooden spatula and gently turn over the rice to distribute the peas and onions and release some steam.

■ Serve hot in small individual bowls. If not serving immediately, place a clean kitchen towel over the saucepan before replacing the lid to absorb the steam and keep the rice fluffy.

MATSUTAKE GOHAN
■ RICE AND MUSHROOMS ■

SERVES 4

LUSCIOUSLY FLAVORED, slightly crisp *matsutake* mushrooms create a luxurious rice to grace a special meal. Any other mushrooms can be used.

6 ounces fresh *matsutake, shiitake,*
   oyster or medium cup mushrooms
1 3/4 cups Japanese rice

2 1/4 cups water
1 1/2 teaspoons salt

WIPE MUSHROOM and trim away any tough stems. Cut into thin slices.

■ Put the rice in a deep saucepan. Place it in the sink under running cold tap. Stir the rice carefully in the water with your hand or a wire whisk, allowing the water to overflow until it becomes almost clean. Drain the rice and return to the saucepan. Add 2 1/4 cups water and leave to soak for 1 hour during which time the rice will have absorbed some of the water, partially softening the grains.

■ Add the mushrooms and salt. Stir gently and cover with a tight lid. Do not remove the lid throughout the remaining cooking and final steaming process. Bring very quickly to a boil over a high heat. Steam will appear around the edge of the lid when boiling point is reached. Reduce the heat and simmer very gently for 15 minutes. Turn up the heat to its highest for 10 seconds then turn off the heat and leave the rice to stand on the stove to steam in its own heat for 10 minutes.

■ Dampen a bamboo rice paddle or wooden spatula and gently cut into the rice to release some steam before serving. If not serving immediately, place a clean kitchen towel over the saucepan before replacing the lid to absorb the steam and keep the rice fluffy.

■ Serve hot in small individual bowls.

TAKENOKO MESHI
▪ RICE AND BAMBOO SHOOTS ▪

SERVES 4

THE FRESH earthy flavor and crispness of bamboo shoots adds an interesting dimension to plain rice. Canned bamboo shoots are not quite so good, but may be substituted in this recipe.

▪
about 8 ounces fresh or canned
   bamboo shoots
1 3/4 cups Japanese rice
▪

▪
2 1/4 cups water
1 1/2 teaspoons salt

▪

IF USING fresh bamboo shoots, wash well, cover with lightly salted cold water and bring to a boil. Simmer for about 30 minutes, or until tender. Drain and remove skin. Cut into thin slices about 1/2-inch wide by 1 1/2-inches long. If using canned bamboo shoots, drain and cut into similar-sized pieces.

▪ Put the rice in a deep saucepan. Place it in the sink under a running cold tap. Stir the rice carefully in the running water with your hand or a wire whisk, while allowing the water to overflow until it becomes almost clean. Drain the rice and return to the saucepan. Add the water and leave to soak for 1 hour during which time the rice will have absorbed some of the water, partially softening the grains.

▪ Add the bamboo shoots and salt. Gently stir and cover with a tight lid. Do not remove the lid throughout the remaining cooking and final steaming process. Bring very quickly to a boil over a high heat. Reduce the heat and simmer very gently for 15 minutes. Turn up the heat to its highest for 10 seconds, then turn off the heat and leave the rice to stand on the stove to steam in its own heat for 10 minutes.

▪ Dampen a bamboo rice paddle or wooden spatula and gently cut into the rice to release some steam before serving. If not serving immediately, place a clean kitchen towel over the saucepan before replacing the lid to absorb the steam and keep the rice fluffy.

▪ Serve hot in small individual bowls.

SHOGA MESHI
■ GINGERED RICE ■

SERVES 4

WHEN I first cooked this rice I wondered why I hadn't done so sooner! The tangy pieces of ginger transform plain rice into a gourmet delight.

■
1 3/4 cups Japanese rice
2 1/4 cups water
■

■
2-inch piece of fresh ginger root
1 1/2 teaspoons salt
■

PUT THE rice in a deep saucepan. Place it in the sink under a running cold tap. Stir the rice carefully in the water with your hand or a wire whisk, while allowing the water to overflow until it becomes almost clean. Drain the rice in a colander or sieve and return to the saucepan. Add water and leave to soak for 1 hour during which time the rice will have absorbed some of the water, partially softening the grains.

■ Cut away any damaged parts from the ginger Cut into matchsticks and soak in cold water for 30 minutes.

■ Add the ginger and salt to the rice. Gently stir and cover with a tight lid. Do not remove the lid throughout the remaining cooking and final steaming process. Bring very quickly to a boil over a high heat. Steam will appear around the edge of the lid when boiling point is reached. Reduce the heat and simmer very gently for 15 minutes. Turn up the heat to its highest for 10 seconds, then turn off the heat and leave the rice to stand on the stove to steam in its own heat for 10 minutes.

■ Dampen a bamboo rice paddle or wooden spatula and gently cut into the rice to release some steam before serving. If not serving immediately, place a clean kitchen towel over the saucepan before replacing the lid to absorb the steam and keep the rice fluffy.

■ Serve hot in small individual bowls.

NORI-CHAZUKE
▪ RICE, GREEN TEA AND
SEAWEED ▪

I WAS rather disconcerted when first served this dish to see a pot of tea picked up and emptied into my rice bowl, not realizing that this was the correct procedure. *Nori-chazuke* is also an informal and popular way of finishing off any rice left in one's bowl after a meal. Just pour hot *ocha* (Japanese green tea) over your rice then sprinkle over some *nori goma-shio* (see page 69) or crumble over a crispy piece of *ajitsuke-nori* seaweed. *Nori-chazuke* is considered beneficial in helping to counteract the more unfortunate consequences of an evening of heavy drinking.

MOCHI

MOCHI SYMBOLIZE long life and wealth and are traditionally eaten on important festive occasions, including the New Year. *Mochi* are made of a very glutinous rice which is steamed, pounded into a paste, rolled out like pastry, then cut into small squares, circles or rectangular cakes. When fried or grilled, the *mochi* puff up to almost double their size with a crisp, golden surface and a sticky, glutinous inside.

Large quantities of *mochi* were traditionally made for special occasions and pounding the *mochi* rice was very hard work. The hot steamed rice was put into a large log which was hollowed out to form a smooth bowl, and then pounded with a log until the crushed grains became a smooth, homogenous mass.

Pounding the rices
My hands are chapped.
Tonight my young prince
Will take them and sigh.

ANON

Mochi are very arduous and difficult to make, and with the exception of a few rural farmhouses, nobody makes their own *mochi* in Japan these days. Commercially made *mochi* are excellent and an unopened package lasts for months. *Mochi* can be grilled or fried, then either dropped into a bowl of hot *miso* soup; wrapped in paper-thin *nori* seaweed; sprinkled with a little soy sauce or, as in the following recipe, *mochi dengaku,* topped with a tasty *miso* paste.

MOCHI DENGAKU
■ GRILLED STICKY RICE CAKES
WITH SOY BEAN PASTE ■

SERVES 4

CHEWY RICE cakes with a tasty topping named after the popular *dengaku* open-air musical entertainments.

■

2 tablespoons *aka miso*
   (red soy bean paste)
1 teaspoon *mirin* (sweet rice wine)
teaspoon *sake* (fortified rice wine)

■

1 teaspoon egg yolk
2 teaspoons superfine sugar
4 cakes of *mochi*
toasted white sesame seeds

■

IN A bowl, mix together *miso, mirin, sake,* egg yolk and sugar.
■ Place *mochi* well apart on an oiled baking tray. Broil on both sides under a moderate heat for a few minutes until they are puffed up and golden-brown. Take care not to burn them.
■ Spread the *miso* mixture over the top of the *mochi* and sprinkle over a few sesame seeds. Return to the broiler and cook until the *miso* is bubbling a little and has dried on the top. Divide the *mochi* among 4 small serving plates and serve immediately.

DONBURI

A *donburi* is a large porcelain bowl which has given its name to the hot rice dishes served in it. Many Japanese restaurants serve *donburi* and, as uneaten rice is never wasted in Japan, it is also a popular lunch or snack at home, being very quickly made from leftover rice topped with whatever tasty morsels are around. The following are three classical vegetarian *donburi* dishes.

KITSUNE DONBURI
▪ FRIED SOY BEAN CURD WITH SPRING ONIONS AND RICE ▪

SERVES 4

BECAUSE OF the fox-colored *aburage* it contains, this dish is named after *kitsune*, the Japanese fox. *Kitsune* was considered to be a creature of magical powers and Japanese farmers believed that if they hunted the fox they would be punished. *Kitsune donburi* makes a simple light meal or snack.

▪
4 sheets of *aburage* (flat, fried
   soy bean curd)
4 spring onions
1 cup water
▪

▪
4 tablespoons *mirin* (sweet rice wine)
4 tablespoons Japanese soy sauce
hot, cooked rice made with
   1 3/4 cups rice
▪

PUT THE *aburage* in a bowl. Pour over boiling water to remove excess oil, then drain. Cut *aburage* in half lengthwise, then cut across into strips about 1/2-inch wide.

▪ Remove roots and any damaged parts from the spring onions. Wash well and shred finely, diagonally.

▪ Put water, *mirin* and soy sauce into a saucepan. Add *aburage*, bring to a boil and simmer for 10 minutes, or until most of the liquid has been absorbed.

▪ Divide the hot rice among 4 *donburi* or medium-sized bowls. Top with *aburage*, sprinkle over the spring onion and serve immediately.

TAMAGO DONBURI

■ RICE TOPPED WITH SOFT EGG SOY BEAN CURD AND ONIONS ■

SERVES 4

THIS FAVORITE, protein-rich, nourishing dish makes an enjoyable light meal on its own.

■

2 sheets of *aburage* (flat, fried
   soy bean curd)
6 spring onions
1 cup water
4 tablespoons *mirin* (sweet rice wine)

■

4 tablespoons Japanese soy sauce
8 eggs
hot cooked rice made with
   1 3/4 cups rice

■

PUT THE *aburage* in a bowl and pour over boiling water to remove excess oil then drain. Cut *aburage* in half lengthwise, then cut across into strips about 1/2-inch wide.

■ Remove roots and any damaged parts from the spring onions and wash well. Cut four of the onions into 1/2-inch lengths. Shred remaining 2 onions very finely, diagonally.

■ Put the water, *mirin* and soy sauce into a saucepan. Add *aburage* and the 1/2-inch onion lengths and simmer for 2 minutes.

■ Beat eggs and add to the *aburage* mixture. Cook very slowly, with the lid on, until the eggs are only just set. Do not overcook the eggs.

■ Divide the rice among 4 *donburi* or medium-sized bowls. Spoon over the hot egg mixture. Sprinkle over the shredded spring onions and serve immediately.

Ⓥ TEMPURA DONBURI
■ RICE WITH DEEP-FRIED VEGETABLES IN CRISPY BATTER ■

SERVES 4

GOLDEN CRISP-COATED vegetables, soft rice and a tasty sauce make a delightful light meal.

■
12 pieces of *tempura*
   (see pages 119-121)
4 tablespoons *mirin* (sweet rice wine
4 tablespoons Japanese soy sauce

■
1 cup water
1 teaspoon *wasabi* paste
   (Japanese horseradish paste)
hot, cooked rice made with
   1 3/4 cups rice

■   ■

COOK THE *tempura* according to the recipe on pages 119-121.

■ Mix *mirin,* soy sauce and water together in a saucepan and heat to boiling point. Add *wasabi* and mix well.

■ Divide the rice among 4 *donburi* or medium-sized bowls. Top with the tempura. Pour over the soy sauce mixture and serve immediately.

SUSHI

There are an incredible number of *sushi* stalls and bars in Japan ranging from the plushy and expensive to the plain and functional. Most have a long bar lined with stools on which you perch while watching your order of *sushi* being prepared with a great deal of showy dexterity and skill. Many *sushi* restaurants have a delivery service to home or office by bicycle, and the traffic-dodging *sushi* cyclists, peddling shiny lacquered trays of the jewel-like treats, and sporting traditional *happikimonos*, are a colorful sight.

Sushi are exquisitely attractive concoctions made from delicately flavored, sweet-vinegared rice, shaped and stuffed and/or garnished with various tasty morsels. They are not difficult to make and their preparation is less involved than it seems. Fish *sushi* are common in Japan, but there are some delicious vegetarian varieties, the recipes for which follow.

Sushi are eaten cold and can form part of the Japanese lunch box, *bento*. They impart an air of luxury when served instead of plain rice at a meal. They also make an ideal snack or picnic served with frosty, iced *Sapporo* or *Kirin* Japanese beer.

A large serving dish of mixed varieties of *sushi* and *onigiri* (see page 47) served with soy sauce to sprinkle over and fiery green *wasabi* (Japanese horseradish paste) and individual bowls of *miso* soup make a decorative and delicious informal meal.

Sushi rice (*sushi meshi*) can also be mixed with various vegetables, and served without shaping, to make the extremely flavorful and enjoyable rice dish *chirashi zushi* (see page 67).

Always use Japanese rice when making *sushi*.

SUSHI MESHI
■ SWEET-VINEGARED *SUSHI* RICE ■

SERVES 4

SUSHI MESHI is delicately vinegared, slightly sweet rice used as the basis for several *sushi* dishes. This recipe makes sufficient *sushi* meshi to prepare your choice of two *sushi* recipes.

1 3/4 cups Japanese rice
2 1/4 cups water
5 tablespoons *sushi-su* (special
    Japanese rice vinegar
    for making *sushi*)

3 tablespoons superfine sugar
2 teaspoons salt

COOK RICE according to the recipe for plain rice on page 46.

■ While the rice is cooking, put the vinegar, sugar and salt into a saucepan and heat gently while stirring to dissolve the sugar and salt. Cool in the refrigerator.

■ When rice has finished steaming, place it in a wide, shallow container, such as a baking pan, large wide bowl or large serving plate. Sprinkle the vinegar mixture evenly and lightly over the rice. Dampen a wooden rice paddle or spatula and gently turn over the rice to fluff it up and distribute the vinegar mixture. (If you are making *inari zushi* (page 61), this is the time to add the black sesame seeds.)

■ Ideally, at the same time as turning the rice with one hand you should fan the rice quickly with the other hand using a piece of paper, fan or a hair dryer set on cold, until most of the steam disappears. Fanning will cause the rice to become glossy as it cools. It's a good idea to get someone else to fan the rice for you while you are turning it over, or fix the hair dryer in position.

■ Cover the *sushi meshi* with a damp cloth until you are ready to use it in any of the following *sushi* recipes.

INARI ZUSHI
■ STUFFED SOY BEAN CURD ■

MAKES 8 *INARI ZUSHI* TO SERVE 4

ATTRACTIVELY PREPARED golden parcels of *aburage* conceal *sushi meshi* and black sesame seeds. If possible, add the sesame seeds to the hot *sushi meshi* at the same time as the vinegar mixture.

■

sushi meshi made with 14 tablespoons uncooked Japanese rice and 1 tablespoon toasted black sesame seeds (see page 60)
4 sheets of *aburage* (flat, fried soy bean curd)

■

4 tablespoons superfine sugar
4 tablespoons Japanese soy sauce
1 tablespoon *sake* (fortified rice wine)
shoga-ama-zuke (sweet pickled ginger)

■

PREPARE THE *sushi meshi* rice according to the recipe on page 60, adding the sesame seeds to the rice at the same time as the vinegar mixture.
■ Put *aburage* in a bowl. Pour over boiling water to remove excess oil. Drain and leave until cool enough to handle. Cut each *aburage* sheet in half across the shortest width. Taking care not to tear the *aburage*, gently ease open each half to make 8 pouches. Tease open the corners with chopsticks or a teaspoon handle.
■ In a saucepan, put the water, sugar, soy sauce, *sake* and *aburage* pouches. Bring to a boil, then simmer gently, turning and basting the *aburage* in the liquid from time to time, until most of the liquid has been absorbed. Allow to cool, then squeeze out remaining liquid until almost dry.
■ With lightly moistened hands, divide the rice into 8 portions. Fill each *aburage* pouch with a portion of rice, gently pressing to distribute. Fold the open edges of the *aburage* over the rice to enclose, and stand the pouches on their sealed edges.
■ Arrange on small, individual plates and garnish with a little *shoga-ama-zuke*. Serve cold, immediately, or cover with a damp cloth and use within a few hours.

VARIATION

Carrot and *shiitake* mushrooms can be substituted for the sesame seeds in the above recipe.
■ Soak 2 dried *shiitake* mushrooms in warm water for 20 minutes. A small plate or saucer on the mushrooms will keep them submerged. Remove stems and discard. Slice the cap into very fine strips.

- Peel half a carrot and cut into matchsticks.
- Follow the method of the preceding recipe, cooking the *shiitake* and carrot with the *aburage* in the simmering liquid.
- Mix the cooked carrot and mushrooms with the *sushi* rice in place of the sesame seeds before stuffing the *aburage* pouches.

HOSOMAKI
■ THIN *SUSHI* ROLLS ■

MAKES 24 *HOSOMAKI* TO SERVES 4

THESE VISUALLY beautiful and flavorful delights are one of the most popular dishes served in Japanese sushi bars. They are always served 6 pieces to a portion.

sushi meshi (sweet-vinegared rice) made from 14 tablespoons uncooked Japanese rice
1/2 cucumber
2 ounce piece of *takuan* (pickled radish)

2 sheets of *nori* seaweed
1 teaspoon Japanese rice vinegar
wasabi paste (Japanese horseradish paste)
shoga-ama-zuke (sweet pickled ginger)

PREPARE THE *sushi meshi* rice according to the recipe on page 60.

- Wash and dry the cucumber. Cut it in quarters lengthwise. Remove the seeds with a spoon and cut remaining cucumber into matchsticks. Leave on absorbent paper towels to drain off excess liquid.
- Grate the *takuan* pickle on a coarse cheese grater and drain on absorbent paper towels.
- Pass the *nori* seaweed backwards and forwards over a high flame for a few seconds, or briefly toast under the broiler until it becomes a lighter green (unless using sushi *nori* which is pretoasted). Cut each sheet of *nori* in half.
- Add the vinegar to a small bowl of water and use it to moisten your fingers from time to time while making the *sushi*. Do not make your fingers too wet or you will spoil the texture of the rice.
- Spread out a Japanese bamboo rolling mat, *makisu,* with the smooth side uppermost and the bamboo strips running from left to right. Lay a piece of *nori* on the mat. Moisten your hands with the vinegar-water and spread a quarter of the *sushi meshi* rice evenly over the nearest three-quarters of the *nori* sheet, covering it right to the

edges, but leaving uncovered 1-inch at the top and 1/2-inch at the bottom (see illustration 1). Place half of the *takuan* pickle in a line, widthways, across the middle of the rice.

■ Dampen the uncovered top edge of the *nori*. Using the rolling mat as a guide, lift the *nori* and rice in the mat and roll it away from you while pressing the mat firmly around the *sushi*, to make a neat firm cylinder. Try to keep the filling in the center of the roll (see illustrations 2 and 3 below). Complete the roll and leave the *sushi* to rest on its seam for about 10 minutes to settle and seal the edge. Remove the *sushi* from the mat. Dampen a sharp knife and cut the *sushi* roll into 6 pieces. Cover the *sushi* with a damp cloth.

■ Make another *sushi* roll with another quarter of the rice and the remaining *takuan* pickle. Cut into 6 pieces and cover with a damp cloth, as before.

■ Make 2 more *sushi* rolls as above, substituting the cucumber for the *takuan*. Smear a thin line of *wasabi* paste along the cucumber before rolling and cutting as before.

■ Arrange *sushi* on 4 small plates or 1 large serving dish. Garnish with a sliver of *shoga-ama-zuke*. If not using immediately, cover with a damp cloth and use within a few hours.

FUTOMAKI
■ THICK *SUSHI* ROLLS ■

MAKES 8 OR 10 *FUTOMAKI* TO SERVE 4

THESE ARE rather more substantial variations of *Hosomaki.*

■

sushi meshi (sweet-vinegared rice)
   prepared from 14 tablespoons
   uncooked Japanese rice
4 dried *shiitake* mushrooms
1 cup warm water
2 tablespoons Japanese soy sauce
2 tablespoons *mirin* (sweet rice wine)
3 1/2 tablespoons superfine sugar
salt

■

vegetable oil
2 eggs
1/2 cucumber
2 sheets of *nori* seaweed
1 teaspoon Japanese rice vinegar
water
wasabi paste (Japanese
   horseradish paste)
shoga-ama-zuke (sweet ginger pickle)

PREPARE THE *sushi meshi* rice according to the recipe on page 60.

■ Soak the mushrooms in 1 cup warm water for 30 minutes. A saucer or small plate on the mushrooms will keep them submerged. Remove the mushrooms and plate, reserving the soaking water. Cut off hard stems from the mushrooms and discard. Slice the caps very finely. Return mushrooms to the soaking water Add the soy sauce, *mirin*, 3 tablespoons superfine sugar and a pinch of salt. Bring to a boil and simmer until most of the liquid has been absorbed. Drain mushrooms on absorbent paper towels.

■ Lightly oil a frying pan and heat. Beat the eggs with 1/2 tablespoon superfine sugar and a pinch of salt. Pour into the hot frying pan and make an omelet, turning once. Remove carefully on to absorbent paper towels and cut into thin strips about 1/4-inch wide.

■ Cut the cucumber in quarters lengthwise. Remove the seeds with a spoon and discard. Cut cucumber into matchsticks and leave on absorbent paper towels to drain off excess liquid.

■ Pass the *nori* backwards and forwards over a high flame, or briefly toast under a broiler until the color changes to a lighter green (unless using *sushi nori* which is pretoasted).

■ Combine the vinegar and water together in a small bowl and use it to moisten your fingers from time to time while making the *sushi.* Do not make your fingers too wet or you will spoil the texture of the rice.

■ Spread out a Japanese rolling mat, *makisu,* with the smooth side uppermost and the strands of bamboo running from left to right. Lay a piece of *nori* on the mat. Moisten your fingers with the vinegar-water and spread half of the *sushi meshi* rice evenly over the nearest 3/4 of the *nori* sheet, covering it right to the edges, but leaving uncovered 1 1/2-inches at the top and 1/2-inch at the bottom.

■ Arrange half of the egg strips in a line widthwise across the middle of the rice. Lay half of the cucumber in a line next to the egg strips and repeat with a line of half of the mushrooms. Arrange the fillings neatly and close together. Smear a thin line of *wasabi* paste over the cucumber.

■ Dampen the uncovered top edge of the *nori.* Using the rolling mat as a guide (see page 63), lift the *nori* and rice in the mat and roll it away from you while pressing the mat firmly around the *sushi,* to make a neat firm cylinder. Try to keep the fillings in the center of the roll. Complete the roll and leave the *sushi* to rest on its seam for about 10 minutes to settle and seal the edge.

■ Remove the *sushi* from the mat. Dampen a sharp knife and cut the *sushi* roll in half. Cut each half into 4 or 5 slices.

■ Cover the *sushi* with a damp cloth while you repeat the process using the remaining ingredients.

■ Arrange *sushi* on 4 small plates or 1 large serving dish. Garnish with a sliver of *shoga-ama-zuke.* If not using immediately, cover with a damp cloth and use within a few hours.

TEMAKI

■ SEAWEED CORNETS STUFFED WITH *SUSHI* RICE ■

TEMAKI TASTE as delicious as rolled *sushi* but are simplicity itself to make as you don't need to use a rolling mat. They are fairly casually fashioned cones of crisp, wafer-thin sheets of seaweed, partly filled with *sushi* rice and delicious savory morsels. You don't have to be fussy about how neat they are and they're fun to make and eat at an informal meal or picnic. The diners select their own fillings and roll the *temaki* themselves.

■ Prepare the *sushi meshi* rice and fillings of your choice as in the previous 2 recipes and set out in serving dishes.

■ Pass several sheets of *nori* seaweed backwards and forwards over a high flame for a few seconds, or briefly toast under a broiler until the color changes to a lighter green (unless using *sushi nori* which is pre-toasted). Cut the sheets in half and pile on to a serving dish.

■ To make *temaki*, take a piece of *nori* seaweed and put about 2 teaspoons of *sushi* rice on one end. Top with the fillings of your choice, then roll the *nori* over the fillings to form a cornet or cone, with the fillings in the bottom. Eat as it is, or sprinkle over a little soy sauce or top with a sliver of *shoga-ama-zuke* (pickled ginger) or a dab of *wasabi*, Japanese horseradish.

CHIRASHI ZUSHI
■ SWEET VINEGARED RICE WITH MIXED VEGETABLES ■

SERVES 4

FOR YOUR first attempt at *sushi, chirashi zushi* is an easy dish to make as it doesn't need any rolling or shaping. It makes a most delicious meal accompanied by a Japanese soup and a little salad. Vegans may omit the egg.

■

sushi meshi made with
14 tablespoons Japanese rice
4 dried *shiitake* mushrooms
1/4 pound green peas
1 carrot
1/4 pound green beans

1 1/2 teaspoons sugar
2 tablespoons Japanese soy sauce
2 eggs (optional)
salt
vegetable oil
2 packets of *ajitsuke-nori* seaweed

■

PREPARE THE *sushi meshi* rice according to the recipe on page 60.
■ Soak the mushrooms in 2 cups warm water for 30 minutes. A saucer or small plate on the mushrooms will keep them submerged. Drain the mushrooms and lightly squeeze out the water. Use the soaking water in another recipe, such as *Dashi* (page 30). Cut the hard stems off the mushrooms and discard. Slice mushroom caps very finely.
■ Boil the green peas in lightly salted water until only just tender.
■ Peel the carrot and cut into matchsticks.
■ Wash and trim the beans, then slice into 4 or 5 lengths diagonally
■ Put 2 tablespoons water, 1 teaspoon sugar and the soy sauce into a small saucepan. Add mushrooms, beans and carrot and cover with a lid. Bring to a boil. Remove lid and simmer for 2 minutes while stirring. Drain, discarding the liquid.
■ Beat eggs with 1/2 teaspoon sugar and a pinch of salt. Oil and heat a frying pan and make an omelet, turning once. Remove omelet from pan onto absorbent paper towels and cut into fine strips about 1/4-inch wide.
■ Cut *nori* into fine strips about 1/8-inch wide.
■ Fold vegetables carefully into the rice. Divide among 4 individual bowls or 1 serving dish. Arrange egg strips over the top and sprinkle over the *nori*. Serve hot or cold.
■ If not serving immediately, cover the rice with a damp cloth and sprinkle over the egg and seaweed just before serving.

FURIKAKE
▪ SEASONING GARNISH FOR RICE ▪

FURIKAKE ARE delicious, highly flavored seasonings. They are usually sprinkled over plain rice but are also extremely good for giving a lift to egg or vegetable dishes.

GOMA-SHIO
▪ SESAME SEED GARNISH ▪

A DELICIOUS, richly nutty-flavored sprinkle.

▪
14 tablespoons toasted
 white sesame seeds

▪
3 teaspoons fine sea salt

▪

▪

CRUSH THE sesame seeds in a *suribashi* or pestle and mortar until they look like whole wheat flour. Add the sea salt and mix well.
▪ Store in an airtight container.

NORI GOMA-SHIO
■ SEAWEED AND SESAME SEED GARNISH ■

THE ADDITION of seaweed makes this a very flavorful condiment.

■

14 tablespoons toasted black
    sesame seeds
3 teaspoons fine sea salt

■

6 packages of *ajitsuke-nori*
    seaweed

■　　　　　　　　　　　　■

LIGHTLY CRUSH the sesame seeds in a *suribashi* or pestle and mortar, or under a rolling pin, until about half the seeds are crushed.

■ Crush the seaweed into small fragments.

■ Mix all the ingredients together and store in an airtight container, preferably containing a desiccant* to keep the seaweed nice and crisp.

*The climate in Japan is often very humid and many Japanese packaged foods contain desiccants (moisture absorbers). Your package of *ajitsuke-nori* seaweed will contain one. Don't throw it away. I find them very useful to keep various stored foods such as biscuits dry and crisp.

JAPANESE
NOODLES

Almost anywhere you find yourself in Japan you will see more noodle-houses and bars than any other type of restaurant, which is proof enough of their popularity. Even train stations have their noodle bars, many of which have no seating facilities, encouraging the hungry traveler to hurriedly down his steaming bowl of thick white udon noodles and make way for others.

A more tranquil atmosphere pervades the traditional noodle-house, often a flimsy-looking wooden structure with rice paper panels. Usually there is a small area in front reminiscent of "old Japan" with maybe a water wheel turning over a tiny pool of pebbles, or a delicate stream of water falling onto a balanced piece of bamboo, halved lengthwise to form a trough which continuously tips up and down as it fills and empties. The interior is traditional Japanese with rice-straw matting floors, tatami, and simple wooden tables on each of which is a small bamboo box of spicy seasoning. Sometimes the chef can be glimpsed slicing noodles from the fresh handmade dough, surrounded by steaming cauldrons of boiling water into which the noodles are plunged in long-handled wire sieves. Many such chefs are famed for the cut and texture of their noodles and the deliciousness of their noodle soups and dips

As the rush hour dies down in the big cities and towns, portable noodle-stalls appear everywhere and do a brisk trade until about 2 o'clock in the morning, their benches, tables, and animated customers all surrounded and illuminated by rows of large glowing red lanterns. They provide a cheap and sustaining snack in an atmosphere that is so casual, yet magical.

Noodles are eaten any time and almost anywhere in Japan but they are not usually served as one of the dishes at a main meal. There are many types of Japanese noodles, most of which are obtainable in this country, such as somen, *very fine white noodles made from wheat flour;* harusame, *meaning "spring rain" which are fine translucent strands made from rice or potato flour and usually eaten cold in a sweet vinegar dressing (see Japanese salad recipes, page 137); and the green* cha-soba *made with green tea powder and buckwheat flour. The most popular types of Japanese noodles are* udon, *thick and white, made from wheat flour, and* soba, *thin brownish-fawn noodles, made from buckwheat flour.*

A convenient innovation are the individual packages of udon and ramen *noodles which are already partially cooked and come with packets of instant soup bases in various flavors. The noodles are simmered in the soup base and only take 3 minutes to cook. They can be eaten just as they are or, if various goodies are added, such as a few pieces of fried* tofu, *any vegetables you have around and/or an egg, they make a quick, really delicious and satisfying meal at any time (see page 82).*

UDON
■ WHEAT FLOUR NOODLES ■

These thick white noodles are available in two forms: dried, which take about 10 minutes to cook, and partially cooked, which are sold in packages with a sachet of soup-base mix. The following recipes specify the dried variety. If you wish to use partially cooked *udon* noodles, follow the package instructions. You will need 1 package per person.

UDON OSHIRU
■ CLEAR SOUP BASE FOR *UDON* NOODLES ■

SERVES 4

*Makes approximately
3 1/2 cups, sufficient for
14 ounces dried* udon *noodles*

IF USING the dried variety of *udon* noodles you will need to make a quantity of *udon oshiru*. However, it is very easy to make and will keep for 2-3 days in the refrigerator, and several months in the freezer.

■
8-inch piece of *kombu* (kelp seaweed)
4–6 dried *shiitake* mushrooms
4 cups warm water
4 spring onions
1 carrot
1/2 ounce *tororo-kombu* seaweed
■

■
1 1/2 tablespoons *mirin* (sweet rice wine)
2 tablespoons *sake* (fortified rice wine)
salt
■

DO NOT wash the *kombu*, the powdery patches contain much of the flavor. Dust off any sand with a dry cloth. With scissors, cut the *kombu* 3/4 of the way through in 3 or 4 places.

■ In a large saucepan, soak *kombu* and mushrooms in the water for 3 hours. A small plate or saucer will keep the mushrooms submerged. Remove plate and bring to just below a boil very slowly. Remove *kombu* just below boiling point.

■ Meanwhile, cut the roots and any damaged leaves from the onions. Wash well and roughly chop into 1-inch pieces.

- Peel the carrot and roughly slice into 1/2-inch slices.
- Add *tororo-kombu*, spring onions and carrot to the soup base. Bring to a boil and simmer for 15 minutes. Add soy sauce, *mirin* and *sake* and simmer for 2 minutes. Salt to taste. Strain through a sieve, squeezing out the juice.

KITSUNE UDON
■ FOX NOODLES ■

SERVES 4

THIS POPULAR dish is named after the Japanese fox, *kitsune*, who appears in Japanese folklore as often as in English and European. *Kitsune* is considered to be a very crafty creature, who is extremely fond of *aburage*.

■

14 ounces dried *udon* noodles
about 3 1/2 cups *udon oshiru*
    clear soup base, (see page 72)
4 spring onions
4 sheets of *aburage* (flat, fried
    soy bean curd)

1 cup water
4 tablespoons *mirin* (sweet rice wine)
4 tablespoons Japanese soy sauce
schichimi-togarashi (Japanese
    seven-spice pepper)

■   ■

BRING PLENTY of water to a boil in a large saucepan. When boiling rapidly, add the *udon* noodles and return to a boil. Fast simmer for about 10 minutes, or until the noodles are just cooked (*al dente*). Drain and plunge noodles into cold water, stirring gently to separate the strands. Drain and set aside.

- Trim roots and any damaged leaves from the spring onions. Wash well and slice very finely, diagonally.
- Put *aburage* in a bowl and pour over boiling water to remove excess oil. Drain.
- Put water, *mirin* and soy sauce into a saucepan. Add *aburage* and bring to a boil. Simmer for about 10 minutes, or until most of the liquid has been absorbed, turning the *aburage* from time to time. Fold each piece of *aburage* in half and set aside.
- Bring *udon oshiru* to boiling point in a large pan. Immerse noodles for a few seconds to heat through, divide noodles among 4 *udon* bowls or medium-sized bowls.
- Place 1 piece of *aburage* in each bowl. Sprinkle over the spring onions. Ladle over the *udon oshiru* and serve immediately with *schichimi-togarashi* to sprinkle over the noodles.

TSUKIMI UDON
■ MOON-VIEWING NOODLES ■

SERVES 4

THE GOLDEN, round egg yolk of the poetically named moon-viewing noodles is supposed to resemble the full harvest moon.

14 ounces dried *udon* noodles
about 3 1/2 cups *udon oshiru*
    (clear soup base, see page 72)
4 spring onions

1/2 sheet of *nori* seaweed
4 eggs
schichimi-togarashi (Japanese
    seven-spice pepper)

BRING PLENTY of water to a boil in a large saucepan. When boiling rapidly, add the *udon* noodles and return to a boil. Fast simmer for about 10 minutes, or until noodles are just cooked. Drain and plunge noodles into cold water, stirring gently to separate the strands. Drain and set aside.

■ Trim roots and any damaged leaves from the spring onions. Wash well and slice very finely, on the diagonal.

■ Pass the *nori* through a high flame for a few seconds, or lightly broil until the color changes to a lighter green. Cut into 4 pieces.

■ Bring *udon oshiru* to boiling point in a large saucepan.

■ Immerse noodles in boiling water for a few seconds to heat through, and drain.

■ Divide noodles among 4 *udon* bowls or medium-sized bowls. Sprinkle over the spring onion. Make a hollow in the noodles with a spoon and gently break an egg into it, taking care not to break the yolk. Carefully ladle over a boiling *udon oshiru*, in which the egg will lightly poach. Place a square of *nori* seaweed on each bowl without covering the egg yolk. Serve immediately with *schichimi-togarashi* to sprinkle over the noodles.

NATTO UDON

■ *UDON* NOODLES WITH FERMENTED SOY ■

SERVES 4

RICH IN calcium, protein and the B vitamins, including B[12], *natto* is made by fermenting soy beans in malt. Its strong malty flavor and gluey threads can be off-putting to the uninitiated, but it is considered a delicacy by those who acquire the taste. *Natto* is usually sold in small, individual plastic packages which also contain packets of soy sauce and searingly hot Japanese mustard. These can be mixed into the *natto* before eating, if desired.

■

14 ounces dried *udon* noodles
about 3 1/2 cups *udon oshiru*
   (clear soup base, see page 72)
4 spring onions

■

5 ounces *natto* (fermented soy beans)
4 packets of *ajitsuke-nori* seaweed
Japanese or English prepared mustard

■

BRING PLENTY of water to a boil in a large saucepan. When boiling rapidly, add the *udon* noodles and return to a boil. Fast simmer for about 10 minutes, or until noodles are just cooked. Drain and plunge noodles into cold water, stirring gently to separate strands. Drain and set aside.

■ Trim roots and any damaged leaves from the spring onions. Wash well and slice very finely, on the diagonal.

■ Bring *udon oshiru* to boiling point in a large saucepan.

■ Immerse noodles in boiling water for a few seconds to heat through, and drain. Divide noodles among 4 *udon* bowls or medium-sized bowls. Put the *natto* on top. Sprinkle over the spring onions. Carefully ladle over the *udon oshiru*. Crush a package of *ajitsuke-nori* over each bowl and top with 1/4 teaspoon of mustard. Serve immediately with extra mustard served separately.

NABE YAKI UDON
■ *UDON* NOODLES, FRIED *TOFU* AND VEGETABLES IN SMALL CASSEROLES ■

SERVES 4

A WARMING, hearty, one-pot dish for chilly winter days. A complete meal traditionally served in small, individual, lidded casseroles, *donabe*. Vegans may omit the eggs.

■

about 10 ounces fresh *tofu*
   (soy bean curd)
4 dried *shiitake* mushrooms
14 ounces dried *udon* noodles
4 spring onions
vegetable oil for deep-frying
1 cup *dashi* (see page 30)
4 tablespoons *mirin* (sweet rice wine)

■

4 tablespoons Japanese soy sauce
8 pieces of *tempura*
   (see pages 119-121)
3 1/2 cups *udon oshiru*
   (clear soup base, see page 72)
4 eggs
schichimi-togarashi (Japanese
   seven-spice pepper)

WRAP THE *tofu* in a kitchen towel for 30 minutes to drain excess water.

■ Soak the dried *shiitake* mushrooms in warm water for 30 minutes. A small plate or saucer on top will keep them submerged. Remove stems and discard. Cut a decorative star in the top of each mushroom cap. Keep the water the mushrooms were soaked in to make Vegetarian *Dashi* (see page 30).

■ Bring plenty of water to a boil in a large saucepan. When boiling rapidly, add the dried *udon* noodles and return to a boil. Fast simmer for about 10 minutes, or until noodles are just cooked. Drain and plunge noodles into cold water, stirring gently to separate the strands. Drain and set aside.

■ Remove the roots and any damaged parts from the spring onions. Wash well and slice very finely, on the diagonal.

■ Cut *tofu* on the diagonal into 4 large triangles. Heat the oil to 350°F and deep-fry *tofu* for about 3 minutes or until golden and crisp on the outside. Drain on paper towels.

■ Put the *dashi*, *mirin* and soy sauce into a saucepan. Add mushrooms and simmer for 15 minutes, until most of the liquid has been absorbed, turning the mushrooms over from time to time.

■ Preheat oven to 350°F.

■ Cook *tempura* according to the recipe on pages 119-121. Drain on absorbent paper towels.

■ Bring *udon oshiru* to a boil.

76
■

- Put noodles in a strainer and immerse in boiling water for a few seconds to heat through, then drain.
- Divide noodles among 4 large bowls. Arrange the *tofu* and mushrooms attractively on top. Ladle over the *udon oshiru*. Using a spoon, make a small hollow in the noodles and break in an egg. Cover and put in the oven for 2-3 minutes. Just before serving sprinkle over the spring onions and arrange the *tempura* on top without covering the egg or mushrooms. Serve with *schichimi-togarashi*.

TEMPURA UDON
■ *UDON* NOODLES WITH DEEP-FRIED VEGETABLES ■

SERVES 4

SOFT STRANDS of thick *udon* noodles appetizingly topped with crisp golden-coated vegetables create a tempting light meal.

■
14 ounces dried *udon* noodles
3 1/2 cups *udon oshiru*
   (clear soup base, see page 72)
■

■
4 spring onions
8 pieces of *tempura* (pages 119-121)
■

BRING PLENTY of water to a boil in a large saucepan. When boiling rapidly, add the *udon* noodles and return to a boil. Fast simmer for about 10 minutes, or until noodles are just cooked (*al dente*). Drain and plunge noodles into cold water, stirring gently to separate the strands. Drain and set aside.

- Trim the roots and any damaged leaves from the spring onions. Wash well and slice very finely, on the diagonal.
- Cook the *tempura* according to the recipe on pages 119-121.
- Bring *udon oshiru* to a boil.
- Immerse noodles in boiling water for a few seconds to heat through, then drain. Divide noodles among 4 *udon* bowls or medium-sized bowls. Carefully ladle over the *udon oshiru*. Sprinkle over the spring onions. Top each bowl with 2 pieces of *tempura* and serve immediately, while the *tempura* is hot and crisp.

SOBA
■ BUCKWHEAT NOODLES

Soba noodles have a rich, delicious flavor and a fairly firm texture. They are made from buckwheat flour which gives them their beige color. *Soba* can be eaten hot or cold. When chilled they make a wonderfully refreshing summer meal served with a Japanese salad and fresh fruit.

SOBA OSHIRU
■ CLEAR SOUP BASE FOR *SOBA* NOODLES ■

SERVES 4

*Makes approximately
3 1/2 cups, sufficient for
14 ounces dried* soba *noodles*

IF LIKED, you can prepare this soup base in advance and either freeze for several months, or store in the refrigerator for 2-3 days.

■

8-inch piece of *kombu* (kelp) seaweed
4–6 dried *shiitake* mushrooms
4 cups warm water
4 spring onions
1 carrot
1/2 ounce *tororo kombu* seaweed
5–6 tablespoons Japanese soy sauce

■

1 1/2 tablespoons *mirin*
   (sweet rice wine)
2 teaspoons *sake* fortified rice wine)
1 teaspoon *wasabi* paste
   (Japanese horseradish paste)
salt

■

DO NOT wash the *kombu*, the powdery patches contain much of the flavor. Dust off any sand with a dry cloth. With scissors, cut the *kombu* three-quarters of the way through in 3 or 4 different places.

■ In a large saucepan, soak *kombu* and mushrooms in the warm water for 3 hours. A small plate or saucer will keep the mushrooms submerged. Remove plate and slowly bring to just below boiling, then remove *kombu*.

■ Meanwhile, cut the roots and any damaged leaves from the spring onions. Wash well and roughly chop into small pieces.

■ Wash carrot and roughly chop into small pieces.

■ Add *tororo kombu*, spring onions and carrot to the *shiitake* mushrooms. Bring to a boil and simmer for 15 minutes. Add soy sauce, *mirin* and *sake* and simmer for another 2 minutes, adding salt to taste if necessary. Strain well through a colander or sieve. Add *wasabi* paste and mix well.

TEMPURA SOBA
■ BUCKWHEAT NOODLES WITH DEEP-FRIED VEGETABLES ■

SERVES 4

DELICIOUS NUTTY-FLAVORED buckwheat noodles topped with golden crispy-coated vegetables for a light meal that's a special treat.

14 ounces dried *soba* noodles
12 pieces of *tempura*
(deep-fried vegetables)

3 1/2 cups *soba oshiru*
(clear soup base, see page 72)
schichimi-togarashi (Japanese seven-spice)

BRING PLENTY of water to a boil in a large saucepan. When boiling rapidly, add the *soba* noodles and return to a boil. Add a mug of cold water and bring to a boil again. Purists would repeat twice more with another 2 mugs of cold water. Fast simmer for about 10 minutes, or until the noodles are just cooked (*al dente*). Drain and plunge the noodles into cold water, stirring gently to separate the strands. Drain and set aside.

■ Cook the *tempura* according to the recipe on pages 119-121.
■ Bring *soba oshiru* to a boil.
■ Immerse noodles in boiling water for a few minutes to heat through, then drain. Divide noodles among 4 bowls. Top each serving with 2 pieces of *tempura*. Ladle over a boiling *soba oshiru* and serve immediately with *schichimi-togarashi*.

ZARU SOBA
■ CHILLED BUCKWHEAT NOODLES ■

SERVES 4

ZARU SOBA is one of our favorite summer dishes. It is pure heaven on a hot day served with a bowl of delicate, clear Japanese soup, some chilled silken *tofu* or a few pieces of *tempura* (deep-fried vegetables in a crispy batter), which can also be dunked into the dipping sauce—delicious! It is traditionally served in square wooden *zaru soba* dishes, but woven bamboo plates or chilled china plates are also used.

■

10.6 fluid ounce bottle of *Yamasa* brand *tempura-tsuyu* (dipping sauce)
14 ounces dried *soba* noodles
4 spring onions

2-inch slice of fresh *daikon* (giant radish), optional
1 teaspoon *wasabi* paste (Japanese horseradish paste)
4 packets of *ajitsuke-nori* seaweed

■

PUT *TEMPURA-TSUYA* in the refrigerator to chill.

■ Bring plenty of water to a boil in a large saucepan. When boiling rapidly, add the *soba* noodles and return to a boil. Add a mug of cold water and bring to a boil again. Purists would repeat twice more with another 2 mugs of cold water. Fast simmer for about 10 minutes, or until the noodles are just cooked (*al dente*). Drain noodles and plunge into a large bowl or saucepan of cold water under a running tap. Stir gently to separate the strands until the noodles are cold. Drain, cover and chill in refrigerator.

■ Remove roots and any damaged parts from the spring onions. Wash well and shred finely, on the diagonal.

■ Grate the *daikon* and leave on absorbent paper towels to drain. Do not squeeze.

■ Neatly arrange a mound of spring onions, a dab of *wasabi* and a small, cone-shaped portion of grated *daikon* on each of 4 small dishes.

■ Pour the chilled *tempura-tsuya* into 4 small bowls.

■ Cut the *ajitsuke-nori* into fine strips with scissors.

■ Divide noodles among 4 square, wooden *zaru soba* dishes. Sprinkle *nori* strips over each portion.

■ Serve each diner with a dish of noodles, a bowl of *tempura-tsuya* and a small plate of garnish (*wasabi*, grated *daikon* and shredded spring onion).

■ To eat, mix the *wasabi*, grated *daikon* and spring onions into the *tempura-tsuyu* dipping sauce. With chopsticks, take a portion of noodles and submerge them into the dipping sauce before eating.

YAKISOBA
■ FRIED NOODLES WITH VEGETABLES ■

SERVES 4

THE JAPANESE have always borrowed ideas from the food of other nations, juggling them around to create something uniquely their own. This unlikely sounding fusion of Chinese noodles, Western-style sauces and Japanese seaweed is a delicious example.

■ Vast quantities of *yakisoba* are consumed every day in Japan. Buy genuine fresh egg noodles from a Chinese or Japanese shop. They look like skeins of beige wool.

■

12 ounces fresh Chinese egg noodles
5 tablespoons vegetable oil
salt and pepper
3 cups finely shredded firm white
    Dutch cabbage
2 or 3 carrots

■

1 onion
5 tablespoons Japanese *tonkatsu* sauce
3 tablespoons tomato ketchup
aonori-ko (powdered seaweed)
4 fried eggs, optional

■

BRING A large pan of water to a boil. Add noodles and return to a boil, stirring to separate the strands. Fast simmer for 6-7 minutes, or until just done (*al dente*). Drain thoroughly.

■ Heat a large, dry, nonstick saucepan. Add 3 tablespoons of the oil and allow it to become hot. Add noodles and stir-fry for 2-3 minutes, adding 1 teaspoon each salt and pepper. Tip onto a large serving dish to allow steam to escape.

■ Peel the carrots and cut into matchsticks.

■ Peel and finely slice the onion.

■ Heat a large, dry, nonstick saucepan. Add the remaining oil and allow to become hot. Add onion, cabbage and carrot. Stir-fry, adding 1/2 teaspoon each salt and pepper, for 3-4 minutes or until the onion is translucent. Add noodles and stir-fry for 1 minute.

■ Mix together *tonkatsu* sauce and tomato ketchup, then stir into the noodles. Stir-fry for another 1 minute.

■ Arrange noodles on 4 plates. Dust with ao*nori-ko* and serve. If desired, top with a fried egg, also dusted with *aonori-ko*.

VARIATION

Slice 1/2 block (about 3 1/2 to 4 ounces) of smoked *tofu* into thin slices. Cut into small pieces and fry in vegetable oil until slightly crisp and golden. Stir into the noodles when adding sauces.

'INSTANT' RAMEN
■ PARTIALLY COOKED NOODLES ■

THE BEST possible basis for ultra-quick, wholesome meals are instant *ramen* noodles. They are partially cooked and come in packages with packets of instant clear soup base powder.

I prefer to use Japanese instant *ramen* noodles, but Asian shops sell Taiwanese varieties which are also good. Just check the package to see whether they contain animal products. Unopened packages keep for months and I find them a wonderful standby for unexpected visitors, or when I want to cook something quick yet delicious. They are also very cheap.

CHAN PON MEN
■ INSTANT *RAMEN* NOODLES WITH FRIED SOY BEAN CURD AND BROCCOLI ■

SERVES 2

ANYONE WHO staggers home after a tiring day and makes this super-quick, filling and nourishing meal becomes a lifetime convert. The noodles and vegetables take only 3 minutes to cook and the whole meal can be on the table in less than 20 minutes.

This recipe is just one example of what can be added to *ramen* noodles. Almost any vegetables can be used in any combination, such as shredded green cabbage, Chinese bok choy, sliced mushrooms, sliced leeks, carrot matchsticks, green peas, snow peas, sliced zucchini, diced squash.

■

about 1/2 pound broccoli (1 stalk)
3-4 spring onions
about 10 ounces fresh *tofu*
    (soy bean curd)
vegetable oil for deep-frying
about 2 cups water (or see back
    of package for quantity)

■

2 packages of instant *ramen* noodles
    (containing packets of instant
    soup base)
about 1/2 cup frozen corn, optional
sesame oil or toasted sesame
    seeds, optional

■   ■

WASH AND trim the broccoli and cut into smallish pieces.

■ Trim roots and any damaged parts from the spring onions and wash well. Cut each onion into 3 pieces.

■ Cut *tofu* into 12 equal-sized cubes.

■ Heat oil to 350°F. Drop *tofu* cubes into the hot oil and deep-fry for 3 minutes or until crisp and golden-brown on the outside. Drain on absorbent paper towels.

■ Meanwhile, bring the water to a boil in a medium to large saucepan. Add the broccoli and spring onions. Return to a boil and add the *ramen* noodles. Return to a boil, stirring a little to separate the noodles. Boil for 2 minutes. Add the *tofu* and corn. Boil for 1 minute, then stir in packets of soup base mix.

■ Divide noodles, vegetables, *tofu* and soup between 2 large bowls. Sprinkle over a little sesame oil or a scattering of toasted sesame seeds. Serve immediately.

VARIATION

SERVES 2

Large steaming bowls of *ramen* noodles are sold everywhere in Japan, from traditional restaurants to ramshackle street vendors. The added vegetables and proteins vary considerably, and as well as *tofu*, slices of a sort of fish sausage, *kamaboko*, squid, octopus or meat are often added. A very good high-protein vegetarian alternative is braised gluten. An excellent canned braised gluten, imported from Taiwan and called "mock duck," is available here from health food and Chinese shops.

■

2 packages of instant *ramen* noodles
  (containing packets of instant
  soup base)
vegetables of your choice (see
  introduction to previous recipe)

■

10-ounce can "mock duck"
  braised gluten
2 tablespoons butter or margarine
1/2 crumbly stock cube
  or vegetable bouillon

■

MELT THE butter in a frying pan. Drain the mock duck and add it to the butter. Crumble over the stock cube and fry over a fairly high heat for a few minutes, turning it over occasionally, until hot and browning a little here and there.

■ Meanwhile, cook the 2 packages of *ramen* noodles and vegetables of your choice according to the previous recipe.

■ Divide the noodles, vegetables and soup between 2 large bowls. Arrange the mock duck over the top. Serve immediately.

TOFU AND SOY BEAN DISHES

■ TOFU RYORI ■

Flying over Tokyo at night towards Narita airport, the world's largest and richest city appears as a magical, starry galaxy garlanded with delicate, luminous strings that evolve first into flowing rivers of firefly lights, then into the latest Hondas and Nissans, weaving their way through a neon wonderland.

> *Morning frost.*
> *Mount Fuji*
> *Brushed lightly.*
>
> TANTAN (1674-1761)

An even more magical sight for me was when flying towards Tokyo in a radiant spring morning sky above an endless carpet of mile upon mile of dense white clouds. Suddenly Mount Fuji, luminously pink-gold in the morning sun and delicately ice-capped in lilac-blue, rose like a vision of incomparable beauty from its vast fluffy bed into the clearest of blue skies. Serenely simple in its perfect symmetry, and essentially Japanese, this was the 37th view of the sacred mountain that Hokusai* could never see.

These two visions from on high perfectly symbolize the Japan of today—cherishing its old traditions and values as part of its lifeblood while enthusiastically embracing, even leading, the modern technological world.

Narita airport has many restaurants and in one of these I first had the pleasure of eating what has become one of my favorite dishes, agedashi dofu—*piping hot silky-soft* tofu *in a crisp golden coating served in a delicate clear sauce with a sliver of pink ginger and a scattering of wafer-sliced green onion. Delicious!*

AGEDASHI DOFU
■ CRISP-COATED DEEP-FRIED
TOFU ■

SERVES 4

EVERYONE ENJOYS this deliciously agreeable way of eating *tofu*. If possible, Chinese or Japanese *tofu* sold floating in water, which is available in oriental Asian food shops, should be used for this dish as it is softer and more delicate than the boxed *tofu* usually sold in health food shops.

■

about 10 ounces fresh *tofu*
cornstarch for coating
3 spring onions
vegetable oil for deep-frying

■

10.6 fluid ounce bottle of *Yamasa*
  brand *tempura-tsuyu*
shoga-ama-zuke (sweet pickled
  ginger)

■

WRAP THE *tofu* in a clean kitchen towel for 30 minutes to drain excess water. Cut into 12 equal-sized cubes and coat lightly in cornstarch.

■ Trim roots and damaged parts from the spring onions. Wash well and shred finely, on the diagonal.

■ Heat the oil to 350°F in a large saucepan. Deep-fry the *tofu* for about 3 minutes, until golden and crisp on the outside. Drain on absorbent paper towels.

■ Meanwhile, put the *tempura-tsuyu* into a small saucepan and bring to just boiling.

■ Divide the fried *tofu* among 4 small bowls. Put a slice of *shoga-ama-zuke* on each portion and sprinkle over the spring onions. Pour over the *tempura-tsuyu* and serve immediately.

*HOKUSAI (1760-1849)
A Japanese artist and printmaker who portrayed Mount Fuji from many advantageous viewpoints and in various weather conditions, producing the famous series of Japanese prints known as "The 36 Views of Mount Fuji."

HIYA YAKKO
▪ CHILLED SILKEN *TOFU* ▪

SERVES 4

CHILLED MELTING-LIGHT, silken *tofu* and aromatic tangy ginger—
a favorite dish for hot summer days, and made in minutes.

2 cartons (about 10 ounces each)
 silken *tofu* (soft soy bean curd)
2 spring onions

finely crushed ice, optional
Japanese soy sauce
shoga-ama-zuke (pickled ginger)

CHILL THE *tofu* in the refrigerator for a couple of hours.
▪ Remove roots and any damaged parts from the spring onions.
Wash well and shred very finely, on the diagonal.
▪ Remember that silken *tofu* is very fragile. With a sharp knife, cut
each block of silken *tofu* in half. Carefully lift each half and place
either in chilled bowls filled with finely crushed ice or on chilled
dishes. Sprinkle a little soy sauce over each portion and garnish with
spring onions and a sliver of *shoga-ama-zuke*.

AGE DOFU NO
KARASHI JYOYU KAKE
▪ DEEP-FRIED *TOFU* WITH
MUSTARD-SOY SAUCE ▪

SERVES 4

A RATHER robust dish of golden triangles of fried *tofu* with the punch
of tangy mustard sauce.

about 10 ounces fresh *tofu*
 (soy bean curd)
cornstarch for coating
4 spring onions

2 tablespoons Japanese soy sauce
1 teaspoon Japanese or
 English mustard
vegetable oil for deep-frying

WRAP THE *tofu* in a clean kitchen towel for 30 minutes to drain
excess water. Cut into 4 squares, then cut each square in half on
the diagonal to form 8 triangles in all. Lightly coat each triangle
in cornstarch.

86
▪

■ Trim the roots and any damaged parts from the spring onions. Wash well and shred very finely on the diagonal.

■ In a bowl, mix together the soy sauce, mustard, and 1 tablespoon cold water.

■ In a large saucepan, heat the oil to 350°F and deep-fry *tofu* triangles for about 3 minutes or until golden and crisp on the outside. Drain on absorbent paper towels. Divide *tofu* triangles among 4 bowls or dishes. Drizzle over the sauce and sprinkle over the spring onions.

TOFU DENGAKU
■ BARBECUED OR BROILED *TOFU* TOPPED WITH *MISO* AND SESAME SEEDS ■

SERVES 4

THE POPULAR *tofu dengaku* is sold at Japanese festivals from small, wooden, portable barbecue stalls and is a favorite addition to a vegetarian barbecue.

■
about 20 ounces fresh *tofu* (soy bean curd)
1 cup *aka miso* (red soy bean paste)
1 tablespoon superfine sugar
■

■
1 tablespoon *mirin* (sweet rice wine)
1 tablespoon *sake* (fortified rice wine)
1 egg yolk
toasted white sesame seeds
■

WRAP TOFU in a clean kitchen towel and leave for 30 minutes to drain excess water.

■ Mix *miso*, sugar, *mirin*, *sake* and egg yolk together until smooth.

■ Cut *tofu* into 8 oblongs. Broil under, or barbecue over, a high heat for about 3 minutes on each side.

■ Spread the *miso* mixture over the *tofu*, sprinkle with sesame seeds and cook under a moderate heat, or at the side of the barbecue, until the *miso* bubbles slightly and is dry on top.

■ After cooking, bamboo skewers can be inserted through the *tofu* for easy eating at a barbecue.

INARI MAKI
■ FRIED SOY BEAN CURD ROLLS STUFFED WITH FRESH *TOFU* AND VEGETABLES ■

SERVES 4

INARI MAKI is extremely popular in Japan. It is a delectable, high-protein dish combining soft textures with a touch of crispness in a deliciously flavorful sauce.

■

2 dried *shiitake* mushrooms
4 sheets of *aburage* (flat, fried soy bean curd)
about 5 ounces fresh *tofu*
6 spring onions
1 cup fresh bean sprouts
1-inch piece fresh ginger root

■

1/2 stick celery
1 tablespoon vegetable oil1
1 tablespoon *sake* (fortified rice wine)
salt
2 tablespoons Japanese soy sauce
1 tablespoon *mirin* (sweet rice wine)
2 tablespoons cornstarch

■

SOAK MUSHROOMS in warm water for 20 minutes. A small plate or saucer on the mushrooms will keep them submerged. Drain, reserving the soaking water. Remove hard stems and discard. Lightly squeeze mushroom caps to remove excess water and cut into thin slices.

■ Put *aburage* in a bowl, pour over boiling water and leave for 2-3 minutes. Drain, then carefully squeeze out most of the water. Using sharp scissors and leaving 1 long edge uncut, cut off 3 edges of the *aburage* sheets. Open the *aburage* sheets carefully and flatten without tearing the fourth side.

■ Squeeze the fresh *tofu* in a clean kitchen towel to remove excess water, then crumble until it resembles coarse bread crumbs.

■ Trim roots and any damaged parts from the spring onions, wash well and finely slice. Wash bean sprouts and drain. Trim any damaged parts from the ginger root and cut into matchsticks. Wash celery, remove coarse strings and finely slice.

■ Heat the oil in a pan. Add ginger, spring onions, mushrooms, celery and bean sprouts and stir-fry over a fairly high heat for 2-3 minutes. Add the *sake* and the crumbled *tofu*. Stir-fry for 2-3 minutes to heat through *tofu*, adding a little salt to taste. Remove from pan and divide into 4 portions.

■ Lay out the 4 *aburage* sheets. Put 1 portion of filling on each sheet, spreading it over the nearest two-thirds. Fold a little of the left and right edges of the *aburage* over the filling, then roll it up tightly, away from you, like a jellyroll. Tie each roll up well with cotton thread or they will unroll while cooking.

■ In a pan wide enough to lay the *aburage* rolls side-by side, put 2 cups pint of the mushroom soaking water, the soy sauce and the *mirin.* Bring to a boil. Add *aburage* rolls and simmer with the lid on for 3-4 minutes, turning over the rolls halfway through.

■ Remove rolls onto a plate and drain juice back into pan.

■ Thicken remaining stock with cornstarch dissolved in a little water.

■ Divide rolls among 4 small dishes. With a very sharp knife, cut each roll into 2 or 3 pieces, removing thread. Pour over sauce. Can be served hot or cold.

NIRANEGI TO YAKI DOFU

■ BRAISED DEEP-FRIED *TOFU* WITH LEEKS ■

SERVES 4

HERE THE *tofu* is first deep fried and then braised with leeks in a tasty sauce.

■

about 10 ounces fresh *tofu*
(soy bean curd)
cornstarch for coating
2 young, smallish leeks
1/2 ounce fresh ginger root

■

vegetable oil for deep-frying
4 tablespoons Japanese soy sauce
1 tablespoon *mirin* (sweet rice wine)
1 tablespoon sugar
1 cup water

■

WRAP THE *tofu* in a clean kitchen towel and leave for 30 minutes to drain off excess water. Cut into 12 equal-sized cubes and coat lightly in cornstarch.

■ Remove roots and tough outer leaves from the leeks. Cut 3/4 of the way through into the white part. Wash well under running water. Finely slice.

■ Remove any discolored parts from the ginger and cut into matchsticks.

■ In a large saucepan, heat the oil to 350°F and deep-fry the *tofu* for about 3 minutes, or until crisp and golden on the outside. Drain on absorbent paper towels.

■ Heat about 1 tablespoon oil in a frying pan. Add leeks and ginger and stir-fry for 2-3 minutes. Add soy sauce, *mirin*, sugar and water, stirring a little. Add fried *tofu* and simmer for 2-3 minutes, stirring.

■ Divide among 4 small bowls or dishes and serve immediately.

SHOGA YAKI DOFU
■ GINGERED FRIED *TOFU* ■

SERVES 4

THE FRESH, zesty taste of ginger enlivens this quick-to-make dish.

■

about 10 ounces fresh *tofu*
  (soy bean curd)
cornstarch for coating
2 spring onions
1 1/2-inch piece of fresh ginger root

■

vegetable oil for deep-frying
4 tablespoons Japanese soy sauce
1 tablespoon sugar
1 tablespoon *mirin* (sweet rice wine)
1 cup water

■

WRAP THE *tofu* in a clean kitchen towel and leave for 30 minutes to drain off excess water. Cut into 12 equal-sized cubes and coat lightly in cornstarch.

■ Remove roots and any damaged parts from the spring onions. Wash well and shred finely on the diagonal.

■ Remove any discolored parts from the ginger and cut into matchsticks.

■ In a large saucepan, heat oil to 350°F and deep-fry *tofu* for about 3 minutes, or until crisp and golden on the outside. Drain on absorbent paper towels.

■ Put soy sauce, *mirin*, sugar and water into a saucepan and bring to a boil. Add fried *tofu* and ginger and simmer for 3-4 minutes.

■ Divide the gingered *tofu* among 4 small bowls or dishes, sprinkle over the spring onions and pour over a little of the cooking stock. Serve immediately.

GANMODOKI
■ MOCK DUCK ■

Ganmodoki literally means "mock duck" and is said to resemble wild duck meat in flavor. It is a really delicious and useful protein food made from *tofu*, toasted sesame seeds and vegetables which are mixed together, formed into patties, then deepfried to a golden brown. They can be eaten as they are, either hot or cold, or they can form part of other dishes. *Ganmodoki* is quite different from the mock duck used in the recipe on page 83.

GANMODOKI

■ GOLDEN PATTIES OF FRESH
TOFU AND VEGETABLES ■

SERVES 4 (MAKES 12 PIECES)

THESE SCRUMPTIOUS golden patties, crisp on the outside and full of flavor, make a light yet sustaining meal with salad and a bowl of rice.

about 10 ounces fresh *tofu*
2 dried *shiitake* mushrooms
2 carrots
1 egg

1 teaspoon toasted sesame seeds
1 teaspoon soft
vegetable oil for deep-frying

WRAP THE *tofu* in a clean kitchen towel for 30 minutes to drain excess water. Wrap *tofu* in another clean, dry cloth, then wring it in the cloth to squeeze out as much water as possible.

■ Meanwhile, soak the *shiitake* mushrooms in warm water for 20 minutes. A small plate or saucer on the mushrooms will keep them submerged. Drain. Use the soaking water in another recipe, such as *Dashi* (page 30). Remove stems and discard. Squeeze the mushroom caps to remove some of the water. With scissors, cut into very small pieces.

■ Peel carrots and grate.

■ Lightly beat egg.

■ Mash the *tofu* and knead until it holds together. Add remaining ingredients and knead until it holds its shape when formed into patties. Shape into 12 balls, then lightly flatten to form patties.

■ In a saucepan, heat the oil to 350°F. Deep-fry the *ganmodoki* for about 3 minutes or until a good golden-brown. Drain on absorbent paper towels.

■ Divide among 4 small dishes. Delicious eaten hot or cold.

GANMODOKI ITAME-NI

■ BRAISED GOLDEN PATTIES OF FRESH *TOFU* ■

SERVES 4

DELICIOUS PROTEIN-RICH patties braised in a traditional, flavorful sauce.

■

4 cups water
4 tablespoons Japanese soy sauce
4 tablespoons *mirin* (sweet rice wine)
1 tablespoon sugar

■

■

salt
12 pieces of *ganmodoki*
  (see previous recipe)

■

PUT WATER, soy sauce, *mirin* and sugar into a saucepan. Bring to a boil, adding a little salt to taste. Add the *ganmodoki*. Return to a boil and simmer gently for 4-5 minutes, turning the *ganmodoki* a couple of times.

■ Divide the *ganmodoki* among 4 small bowls or serving dishes and pour over some of the remaining stock.

GANMODOKI TO YASAI NO ITAME-NI

■ *GANMODOKI* AND VEGETABLES IN SWEET VINEGAR SAUCE ■

SERVES 4

IF YOU like sweet and sour dishes, you'll really love this richly colored, very flavorful melange of *ganmodoki* and exotic vegetables braised in a delicate Japanese sweet vinegar sauce.

■

4 dried *shiitake* mushrooms
about 5 ounces fresh or
    canned bamboo shoots
1 carrot, peeled
12 snow peas, trimmed
1 onion, peeled

5 tablespoons soy sauce
2 teaspoons sugar
4 tablespoons Japanese rice vinegar
2 tablespoons *mirin* (sweet rice wine)
2 tablespoons cornstarch
12 pieces of *ganmodoki*
    (see page 92)

■

SOAK SHIITAKE mushrooms in warm water for 20 minutes. A small plate or saucer on the mushrooms will keep them submerged. Drain, reserving soaking water. Discard stalks. Lightly squeeze mushroom caps to remove excess water and cut in half.

■ If using fresh bamboo shoots, wash well, cover with lightly salted cold water and bring to a boil. Simmer for about 30 minutes, or until tender. Drain and remove skin. Cut into thin slices about 1/2-inch wide by 1 1/2-inches long. If using canned whole bamboo shoots, drain and cut into similar-sized pieces.

■ Cut carrot into matchsticks. Cut snow peas in half, on the diagonal.

■ Boil snow peas and carrots in a little lightly salted water for 1 minute, then drain.

■ Peel onion, cut into quarters, then finely slice.

■ Heat oil in a pan and stir-fry onions, mushrooms and bamboo shoots for 2 minutes over a fairly high heat. Add soy sauce, sugar, vinegar and *mirin.* Cook for 1 minute, stirring.

■ Blend cornstarch with 3 cups of reserved mushroom soaking water. Add to the soy sauce and vegetable mixture, stirring. Bring to a boil and simmer for 1 minute. Add *ganmodoki* and simmer for another 2 minutes, turning the *ganmodoki* a couple of time. Stir in carrots and snow peas and simmer briefly to heat through, retaining their slight crispness.

■ Divide among 4 small bowls or dishes and serve hot.

SOY BEANS
■ D A I Z U ■

About a thousand years ago, soy beans were brought by Buddhist monks to Japan from China, where they had been revered for thousands of years as one of five sacred grains. Soy beans make a highly nourishing and healthy addition to your Japanese meal, being very rich in high-quality proteins, vitamins and minerals (including calcium), low in saturated fats and completely free of cholesterol.

DAIZU TO HIJIKI NO NIMONO
SOYA BEANS WITH *HIJIKI* SEAWEED AND GINGER ■

SERVES 4

THE RICH, almost liquorice flavor of *hijiki* seaweed and the aromatic ginger impart delightful and exotic flavors to the nourishing but rather bland soy beans.

1/2 cup dried soy beans
2 ounce *hijiki* seaweed
4-inch piece fresh ginger root

2 tablespoons vegetable oil
2 cups pint *dashi* (see page 30)
shoga-ama-zuke (Ginger pickle)

SOAK SOY beans overnight in plenty of cold water. Drain and put in a lidded saucepan. Cover with plenty of fresh cold water and bring to a boil. Simmer for 1 hour, or until tender but not mushy, topping up with more boiling water as necessary. Drain, soak in cold water until cool, remove the skins, then drain.

■ Meanwhile, soak the *hijiki* seaweed in warm water for 30 minutes, then drain.

■ Remove any discolored parts from the ginger root and grate.

■ Heat oil in a saucepan. Add *hijiki* seaweed and soy beans. Stir-fry for 2-3 minutes. Add *dashi* and bring to a boil. Simmer gently until nearly all the *dashi* has been absorbed.

Divide among 4 small bowls. Squeeze the juice from the grated ginger over each portion and decorate with a sliver of *shoga-ama-zuke*. Can be eaten hot or cold.

DAIZU TO KOMBU NO NIMONO
■ SOY BEANS WITH KELP SEAWEED ■

SERVES 4

A SIMPLE peasant dish rich in proteins and minerals.

3/4 cup dried soy beans
4-inch piece of *kombu* (kelp seaweed)

2 cups *dashi* (see page 30)

SOAK THE soy beans overnight in plenty of cold water.

■ Do not wash the *kombu*; the powdery patches contain much of the flavor. Wipe off any sand with a dry cloth. Using kitchen scissors, cut into 1/4-inch squares.

■ Drain the soy beans and put in a lidded saucepan. Cover with plenty of cold water and bring to a boil. Simmer for 1 hour, or until tender but not mushy, topping up with more boiling water as necessary. Drain the beans and soak in cold water until cool, remove the skins, then drain.

■ Put the soy beans, *dashi* and *kombu* into the saucepan. Bring to a boil and simmer gently until nearly all the *dashi* has been absorbed. Do not fast boil or the *kombu* will become bitter.

■ Arrange in 4 small bowls. Can be eaten hot or cold.

VEGETABLE DISHES

Water I shall draw,
Firewood I shall cut.
Vegetables I shall pick
In the time before
The autumn rainfall.

RYOKAN (1757-L831)

A direct descendant of Samurai *warriors, now in-volved in the peaceful pursuit of* shiitake, *forest-mushroom farming, invited my daughter,* Tian, and me to his mushroom farm. First we met his son's family, now occupying the large old ancestral house in Nara. Our first sight on entering was a pair of fierce-looking Samurai *swords, positioned long ago to be within easy grab-bing distance in the event of unexpected trouble.*

He then took us to his own beautiful house, newly built on family land in the traditional Japanese style. Not far from the house is a large modern building which, on entering, looked more like a laboratory than a farm building. Here the mush-room spores are developed in kanten *jelly (agar-agar), which is kept warm in glassfronted heated cabinets. The resulting mushroom culture is incorporated into small cylindrical plugs made of compressed oak sawdust and nutrients. The plugs are then pushed into holes drilled into logs of the Japanese oak. Outside the logs are piled high in a crisscross structure, each one covered in sprouting* shiitake *mushrooms of varying sizes, the largest of which are continuously harvested.*

Seated on the ground in the sunshine and overseen by the grandmother of the family was a group of Japanese women dressed in traditional slate-blue cotton working clothes. They were unhurriedly packing the freshly harvested mushrooms ready for collection and distribution.

There are now exotic mushroom farms in this country which grow shiitake, matsutake *and other exotic mushrooms (see page 166), and fresh* shiitake *can be bought in most of the larger supermarkets. They are a useful and delicious ingredient in vegetarian cooking as their substantial, almost meaty texture, high protein, vitamin and mineral content and their distinctive, succulent favor more than compensate for the absence of meat.*

On saying sayonara *(goodbye) we were presented with a generous box of freshly picked* shiitake *to take home. That evening we braised them in sake (see following recipe), and ate them with plain white rice, some strips of* ajitsuke-nori *seaweed and crisp salted cucumber pickles. Delicious!*

SHIITAKE NO SAKE NI
■ FRESH *SHIITAKE* MUSHROOMS BRAISED IN *SAKE* ■

SERVES 4

SHIITAKE MUSHROOMS have been revered by the Japanese for centuries for their taste, texture and health-giving properties. They are now thought to help protect from cancer and to reduce cholesterol. This particular dish is very quick to make. Any other mushrooms, including reconstituted dried *shiitake*, may be cooked this way.

■
8 fresh *shiitake* mushrooms
1 tablespoon vegetable oil
2 tablespoons *sake* (fortified rice wine)
■

■
2 tablespoons Japanese soy sauce
2 tablespoons *mirin* (sweet rice wine)
6 tablespoons water
■

Wash the *shiitake* mushrooms and trim off any tough stalks. Slice each mushroom in half.

■ Heat oil in a frying pan and stir-fry mushrooms for 2 minutes.

■ Add remaining ingredients and simmer until most of the liquid has evaporated. Divide among 4 small bowls.

KINOKO NO MIRIN YAKI
■ MIRIN-BARBECUED OR BROILED MATSUTAKE MUSHROOMS ■

SERVES 4

THERE IS an air of mystery about wild *matsutake* which never grow in the same place twice. One autumn a substantial crop of these very expensive mushrooms magically appeared on my father-in-law Taisuke's mountain and were joyously feasted on by the family and fortunate neighbors. The fickle and fancy-free *matsutake* never appeared again. *Matsutake* are available in this country from exotic mushroom farms. Other mushrooms may be cooked this way.

■
4–6 *matsutake* mushrooms
4 tablespoons *mirin* (sweet rice wine)
■

■
1 1/2 tablespoons Japanese
   soy sauce
■

WASH THE mushrooms, remove any hard stalks and slice each mushroom into 3 or 4 slices.

■ Mix together *mirin* and soy sauce in a bowl. Add mushrooms and stir. Leave mushrooms to marinate for 1 hour, turning over in the marinade occasionally.

■ Remove mushrooms and cook under a hot broiler or over a hot barbecue for 2 or 3 minutes on each side, brushing 2 or 3 times with the marinade while cooking. When mushrooms are tender, arrange on 4 small dishes and serve immediately.

MATSUTAKE NO SAKE YAKI
■ SAKE BARBECUED OR BROILED MATSUTAKE MUSHROOMS ■

SERVES 4

LUSCIOUS MATSUTAKE doused in *sake* and cooked over smoky fires evoke the Japanese mountains. Other mushrooms may be cooked this way.

■
4–6 *matsutake* mushrooms
2 teaspoons *mirin* (sweet rice wine)
3 tablespoons Japanese
   soy sauce

■
3 tablespoons Japanese
4 tablespoons *sake*
   (fortified rice wine)

■   ■

WASH THE mushrooms, remove any hard stalks and slice each mushroom into 3 or 4 slices.

■ Mix *mirin*, soy sauce and *sake* in a bowl. Add mushrooms and stir. Leave mushrooms to marinate for 1 hour, turning over in the marinade occasionally.

■ Remove mushrooms and cook under a hot broiler or over a hot barbecue for 2 or 3 minutes on each side, brushing 2 or 3 times with the marinade while cooking. When mushrooms are tender arrange on 4 small dishes and serve immediately.

SHIITAKE TO SHOGA NO TORONI
■ FRESH *SHIITAKE* MUSHROOMS WITH GINGER AND SEAWEED ■

SERVES 4

A quickly cooked and delicious exotic dish. Other mushrooms, including reconstituted dried *shiitake*, can also be used.

■
8 fresh *shiitake* mushrooms
6-inch to 8-inch piece fresh ginger root

■
2 tablespoons Japanese
   soy sauce
4 packets *ajitsuke-nori* seaweed

■   ■

WASH THE mushrooms. Remove hard stems and slice into 3 or 4 slices. Simmer mushrooms in a little lightly salted water for 2-3 minutes, or until just tender. Drain well.

■ Grate ginger root into a bowl and mix with soy sauce and 2 tablespoons cold water. Add mushrooms and stir. Leave to marinate for 5 minutes, turning over the mushrooms once or twice, then drain.

■ Divide among 4 small dishes and crush a packet of *ajitsuke-nori* over each portion.

SHIITAKE NO TORONI
■ BRAISED DRIED *SHIITAKE* MUSHROOMS WITH SESAME OIL ■

SERVES 4

A CLASSICALLY simple yet extremely tasty way to cook dried *shiitake*. Other mushrooms, including fresh *shiitake*, may be cooked this way. Obviously fresh ones will not need soaking.

■

8 dried *shiitake* mushrooms
1 tablespoon vegetable oil
1 teaspoon *sake* (fortified rice wine)

2 tablespoons Japanese soy sauce
4 tablespoons *mirin* (sweet rice wine)
sesame oil

■

SOAK THE mushrooms in warm water for 30 minutes. A small plate or saucer on the mushrooms will keep them submerged. Drain mushrooms, reserving soaking water. Remove stems and discard. Squeeze the mushroom caps a little to remove excess water.

■ Heat the vegetable oil in a frying pan. Add mushrooms and stir-fry for 2 minutes. Add *sake*, soy sauce, *mirin* and 6 tablespoons of the soaking water. Bring to a boil and simmer over a low heat, stirring occasionally, until most of the liquid has evaporated.

■ Divide among 4 small bowls and sprinkle over a little sesame oil.

NASU DENGAKU
■ EGGPLANT BROILED OR BARBECUED WITH SOY BEAN PASTE ■

SERVES 4

PLUMP, SOFT, juicy eggplant topped with a tasty *miso* sauce make a deliciously different vegetable dish. The eggplant in Japan are slightly smaller than those normally sold here. Select smaller eggplant if you can, but any size can be used.

■

2 1/2 tablespoons *aka miso*
   (red soy bean paste)
1 teaspoon sugar
1 teaspoon *mirin* (sweet rice wine)
1 teaspoon *sake* (fortified rice wine)

■

1/2 egg yolk
2 eggplant
salt
vegetable oil for brushing
toasted white sesame seeds

■

MIX TOGETHER the *miso*, sugar, *mirin*, *sake* and egg yolk.

■ Wash the eggplant and cut into 1/2-inch-thick slices. Sprinkle with salt. Leave for 30 minutes to drain, then rinse and pat dry. Brush the eggplant on both sides with oil.

■ To broil: Cook under a high heat on both sides until the eggplant is soft. Spread the *miso* over 1 side of the eggplant and sprinkle over a few sesame seeds. Broil under a moderate heat until the *miso* is bubbling a little and is dry on top.

■ To barbecue: Barbecue one side of the eggplant. Spread the *miso* over the cooked sides and barbecue the uncooked sides until soft.

■ Divide among 4 dishes. Can be eaten hot or cold.

NASU ITAME NI
■ BRAISED EGGPLANT WITH SEAWEED GARNISH ■

SERVES 4

THE INTENSE seafood flavor of *ajitsuke-nori* blends perfectly with succulent, juicy braised eggplant. Select smaller eggplant for this dish if possible.

■

2 small eggplant
salt
4 packets of *ajitsuke-nori* seaweed
2 tablespoons vegetable oil

■

1 3/4 cups *dashi* (see page 30)
1 tablespoon superfine sugar
4 tablespoons Japanese soy sauce

■

WASH THE eggplant, cut off the stalks, cut in half lengthwise, then cut into 1-inch slices. Sprinkle with salt, leave for 30 minutes to drain, rinse and pat dry.

■ With scissors, cut the *ajitsuke-nori* seaweed into fine strips, lengthwise.

■ Heat the oil in a frying pan. Add the eggplant and fry over a medium heat, turning from time to time, until they are just tender. Add the *dashi*, sugar and soy sauce and simmer until the liquid has almost evaporated and the flavor has been absorbed.

■ Divide among 4 small bowls. Sprinkle over the shredded seaweed.

HAKUSAI NO NORI MAKI

■ CHINESE CABBAGE AND SEAWEED ROLLS ■

SERVES 2-4

CABBAGE AND seaweed combine in a very fresh-tasting vegetable dish, decorative to the eye and pleasing to the palate.

12 large outer leaves of
   Chinese cabbage
salt

6 pakets of *ajitsuke-nori* seaweed
Japanese soy sauce

BRING A saucepan of lightly salted water to a boil. Add cabbage leaves and simmer for 3 minutes, or until just tender. Plunge leaves into cold water, then lay them out flat on absorbent paper towels or a clean kitchen towel and pat dry.

■ Take 3 Chinese leaves and spread them out, one on top of the other. Crush 1 1/2 packets *ajitsuke-nori* seaweed evenly over the top. Tightly roll the pile of leaves, starting with the stalk end. Squeeze out excess water while keeping it in a cylinder shape. If you prefer, a Japanese rolling mat, *makisu*, can be used for this (see page 63). With a sharp knife, cut the cylinder into 4 pieces.

■ Repeat with remaining leaves and seaweed. Arrange cut side up between 2-4 small serving dishes. Serve with soy sauce to drizzle over.

HORENSO TO GOMA NO HAKUSAI MAKI
■ CHINESE CABBAGE AND SPINACH ROLLS WITH SESAME ■

SERVES 2-4

ATTRACTIVELY PREPARED concoctions with pleasing contrasts of flavors and colors.

about 5 tablespoons toasted white sesame seeds
salt

10 ounces fresh spinach
4 large Chinese cabbage leaves

CRUSH 4 tablespoons sesame seeds with a good pinch of salt in a *suribashi* or pestle and mortar, or with a rolling pin, until it resembles whole wheat flour.

■ Wash the spinach and remove tough stalks. Bring some lightly salted water to a boil. Add spinach and simmer for 2 minutes. Plunge into cold water, drain, then squeeze out excess water.

■ Bring a saucepan of lightly salted water to a boil. Add cabbage leaves and simmer for 3 minutes, or until just tender. Plunge leaves into cold water, then lay them out flat on absorbent paper towels or a clean kitchen towel and pat dry.

■ Sprinkle each cabbage leaf with crushed sesame seeds then spread the spinach over each leaf. Tightly roll each leaf, starting from the stalk end. Squeeze out any excess water while keeping it in a cylinder shape. If you prefer, a Japanese rolling mat, *makisu*, can be used (see page 63).

■ With a sharp knife, cut each roll into 4 pieces, arrange on small dishes and sprinkle over a few sesame seeds.

KURI TO SHIITAKE NO TORONI

▪ SAUTÉED CUCUMBER AND MUSHROOMS ▪

SERVES 4

SUCCULENT MUSHROOMS and crispy cucumber are stir-fried with *mirin* (sweet rice wine) and soy sauce, then sprinkled with crushed sesame seeds.

▪

1 cucumber
6 fresh *shiitake* mushrooms
2 tablespoons toasted sesame seeds
salt

▪

2 tablespoons vegetable oil
4 teaspoons *mirin* (sweet rice wine)
3 tablespoons Japanese soy sauce

▪ ▪

TRIM THE ends and wash the cucumber. Cut in half lengthwise then into bite-sized pieces about 1 1/2-inches long.

▪ Remove hard stalks from the mushrooms and discard. Wash the mushroom caps and cut into 3 or 4 slices.

▪ Crush the sesame seeds with a good pinch of salt in a *suribashi* or pestle and mortar, or with a rolling pin.

▪ Heat oil in a frying pan. Add cucumber and mushrooms and stir-fry for 3–4 minutes. Add *mirin* and soy sauce. Stir-fry for 2 minutes until the cucumber is cooked but a little crisp.

▪ Arrange in 4 small bowls or dishes and sprinkle over the crushed sesame seeds.

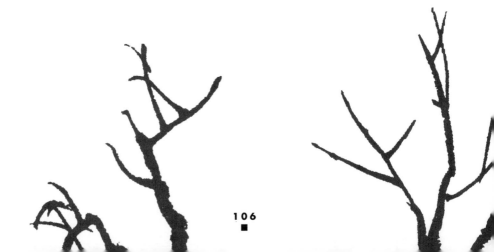

TAKENOKO KIMPIRA
■ BRAISED FRESH BAMBOO SHOOTS ■

SERVES 4

LIKE THE heart of the artichoke, the innermost, gently layered growing surfaces of the tender, newly sprouted bamboo shoot are the most desirable part. This is the simple and classic way to cook this delicacy, but only fresh bamboo shoots should be used for this dish.

■
8 ounces fresh bamboo shoots
salt
1 tablespoon vegetable oil
1 tablespoon Japanese soy sauce
■

■
5 teaspoons *mirin* (sweet rice wine)
schichimi togarashi (Japanese
    seven-spice pepper)
■

WASH BAMBOO shoots well. Cover with lightly salted water and bring to a boil. Simmer for about 30 minutes, or until tender. Drain and remove skin. Slice into 1/2-inch-thick rounds.

■ Heat oil in a saucepan. Add bamboo shoots and stir-fry for 1 minute over a high heat. Add soy sauce and *mirin* and continue to stir-fry over a high heat for another 2-3 minutes, adding a little salt to taste, if necessary.

■ Arrange in 4 small bowls and sprinkle over a little *schichimi-togarashi.*

RENKON KIMPIRA
■ SAUTÉED LOTUS ROOT ■

SERVES 4

THE CRISP fresh texture and flower-like design revealed inside the lotus root provide a most beautiful vegetable dish to grace any meal.

■

8 ounces fresh lotus root
1 tablespoon *su* (Japanese rice vinegar)
1 tablespoon vegetable oil
1 tablespoon Japanese soy sauce

■

5 teaspoons *mirin* (sweet rice wine)
salt
schichimi togarashi (Japanese seven-spice pepper)

■

PUT ENOUGH cold water in a bowl to submerge the lotus root and add the vinegar.

■ Peel the lotus root and cut into 1/8-inch slices. Immedi-ately submerge the lotus root in the vinegar water to pre-vent discoloration.

■ The lotus root slices can be cooked as they are or cut into "flowers" in the following way.

■ Remove 1 piece of lotus root from the vinegar water. Cut away V-shaped wedges all around the edge between the holes, then round off with a sharp knife to form petal shapes. Return immediately to the vinegar water and repeat with remaining lotus root slices.

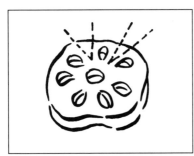 

■ Heat the oil in a saucepan. Drain the lotus root, pat dry with a cloth and add to the hot oil. Stir-fry for 1 minute over a high heat. Add soy sauce and *mirin* and continue to stir-fry over a high heat for another 2-3 minutes, or until the lotus root is tender but still crisp, adding a little salt to taste, if necessary. Arrange in 4 small bowls or dishes, and sprinkle over *schichimi-togarashi*.

JAGAIMO NO SAKE NI
■ SAKE-BOILED POTATOES WITH SEAWEED GARNISH ■

SERVES 4

As PREDOMINANTLY rice-eaters, the Japanese do not consume large quantities of potatoes. They enjoy them in soups or as side dishes, as here where potatoes are elevated to rarer heights with a dash of *sake* and sprinkling of tasty seaweed.

■

4 medium-sized potatoes
3 tablespoons *sake* (fortified rice wine)
2 tablespoons *mirin* (sweet rice wine)
1 3/4 cups water

■

1 1/2 tablespoons Japanese
   soy sauce
4 packets of *ajitsuke-nori* seaweed

■

PEEL POTATOES and cut into bite-sized pieces.

■ Put *sake, mirin,* water and soy sauce into a saucepan. Add potatoes and bring to a boil. Fast simmer, turning the potatoes from time to time, until the potatoes are done and most of the liquid has evaporated.

■ Meanwhile, with scissors, cut the *ajitsuke-nori* seaweed into thin strands.

■ Divide the potatoes among 4 small bowls. Sprinkle shredded *ajitsuke-nori* seaweed over each portion.

TAMANAGI NO TORONI
■ SIMMERED WHOLE ONIONS ■

SERVES 4

THIS SIMPLE dish was part of a meal I was treated to at a dining pavilion in the grounds of an ancient Buddhist temple, where exquisitely prepared vegetarian meals of several courses are ordered in advance and freshly cooked to perfection. One side of the pavilion was fully open to the sublime vistas of the traditional Japanese gardens created many hundreds of years ago to provide a retreat into the meditative tranquillity of idealized mountain scenery, and distance from the everyday world.

■
4 medium-sized onions
3 1/2 cups water
4-inch piece of *kombu* (kelp seaweed)
1 tablespoon *sake* (fortified rice wine)
■

■
1 teaspoon Japanese soy sauce
1/2 teaspoon salt
small edible green sprigs such
    as celery, parsley or watercress
■

PEEL THE onions, keeping them whole, then stand them upright in the bottom of a saucepan.

■ Add water, *kombu*, *sake*, soy sauce, and salt. Bring to a boil. Cover with a lid and simmer very gently until the onions are tender.

■ Remove onions and place in 4 small bowls or dishes. Pour over a little of the cooking stock and decorate with green sprigs.

The radish picker
Points the way
With a radish.

ISSA (1763-1827)

DAIKON DENGAKU
▪GIANT WHITE RADISH WITH SOY BEAN PASTE DRESSING▪

SERVES 4

HUGE WHITE *daikon* radishes, some as thick as an arm, are a common sight in Japanese markets. In this classic recipe, the fresh tasting, succulent *daikon* are enlivened with tasty *miso* sauce and a scattering of citrus peel.

1 pound *daikon* (giant white radish)
4-inch piece of *kombu* (kelp seaweed)
2 tablespoons Japanese soy sauce
2 teaspoons *aka miso*
   (red soy bean paste)

2 teaspoons *shiro miso*
   (white soy bean paste)
2 teaspoons sugar
2 teaspoons *mirin* (sweet rice wine)
2 teaspoons *sake* (fortified rice wine)
grated peel of 1 lemon, Seville
   orange or *yuzu*

PEEL THE *daikon* and cut into 8 rounds about 3/4-inch thick. With a sharp knife cut a star on the top of each round and slightly bevel the hard edges to give a rounded effect (see below). This helps the *daikon* hold their shape while cooking.

▪ Put *daikon* into a saucepan, cover with cold water and bring to a boil. Simmer for 5 minutes. Drain and plunge *daikon* into cold water, then drain again.

▪ Put *daikon* and *kombu* into a saucepan, cover with cold water, add soy sauce and bring to a boil. Simmer until *daikon* is just tender. Do not fast-boil or the *kombu* will give a bitter flavor. Drain, discarding *kombu*.

▪ Put red *miso*, white *miso*, sugar, *mirin* and *sake* into a small saucepan. Heat to just below boiling point. Cook over a low heat, stirring continuously, for 1 1/2 minutes.

▪ Arrange *daikon* on 4 small dishes, pour over the *miso* sauce and sprinkle with citrus peel.

KABOCHA NO TORONI
■ JAPANESE SQUASH SIMMERED IN RICE WINE AND SOY SAUCE ■

SERVES 4

OTHER TYPES of winter squash or pumpkin can be substituted for Japanese squash, but only Japanese or very young squash can be "marbled" in the way described below. If using pumpkin, cut off the hard outer layer, scoop out the seeds and use the softer insides.

about 1 pound Japanese squash
2 1/2 cups water
4 tablespoons *mirin* (sweet rice wine)

1 tablespoon superfine sugar
4 tablespoons Japanese soy sauce
salt

CUT SQUASH in half and remove seeds. Although not essential, some Japanese cooks create a beautiful marbled effect in the following way: casually pare off patches of skin here and there to reveal the green color immediately below the surface skin, then similarly pare off here and there a little deeper to reveal the creamy-colored squash. The varying shades of green and cream contrast with the unpeeled skin to create a beautiful marbled effect. Cut into 1-inch cubes.

■ Put remaining ingredients into a saucepan and bring to a boil. Add squash and return to a boil. Simmer until just tender (*al dente*).

■ Arrange in 4 small bowls, add a little of the cooking liquid and serve immediately.

OKURA NO MISO
■ OKRA WITH *MISO* AND *SAKE* ■

SERVES 4

MISO AND *sake* combine to make a flavorful sauce that complements the glutinous okra. Okra is rich in vitamin A and calcium.

24 fresh okra pods
2 teaspoons *sake* (fortified rice wine)
2 teaspoons *mirin* (sweet rice wine)

2 tablespoons *aka miso*
  (red soy bean paste)
2 teaspoons superfine sugar

WASH OKRA and scrape lightly to remove the downy bloom, then wash well.

■ Bring some lightly salted water to a boil in a saucepan. Add okra and return to a boil. Simmer for about 5 minutes or until just done, then drain.

■ Cut off the stalks, then cut each okra in half, on the diagonal. Mix *sake, mirin, miso* and sugar to a cream. Gently heat in a saucepan while stirring.

■ Toss okra in the *miso* sauce and arrange in 4 small bowls. Serve immediately.

ASUPARAGASU NO TORONI
■ SAKE-COOKED ASPARAGUS WITH SEAWEED GARNISH ■

SERVES 4

PLUMP FRESH asparagus served in a *sake* and *mirin* sauce and topped with shredded seaweed.

■
1 bunch about 12 stalks) of asparagus
4 packets of *ajitsuke-nori* seaweed
salt
■

■
2 teaspoons *sake* (fortified rice wine)
1 tablespoon *mirin* (sweet rice wine)
2 tablespoons Japanese soy sauce
■

WASH ASPARAGUS and cut off tough base of stems.

■ Using scissors, cut *ajitsuke-nori* seaweed into fine strips, lengthwise.

■ Bring a saucepan of lightly salted water to a boil. Slide the hard stalks of the asparagus, but not the tender tips, into the water. Return to a boil and simmer until the hard stalks are only just done (*al dente*) Submerge the tips and simmer for 1 minute, or until just tender. Drain and cut into 1-inch pieces.

■ Put *sake, mirin* and soy sauce into a small saucepan and bring to a boil. Remove from heat.

■ Arrange asparagus in 4 small bowls. Pour over the *sake* sauce and sprinkle over shredded seaweed.

Ⓥ ASUPARAGASU NO TAMAGO SOSU KAKE
■ ASPARAGUS IN EGG SAUCE ■

SERVES 4

INDULGE IN the luxurious flavors of fresh asparagus in a light, creamy sauce scattered with nutty, toasted sesame seeds.

1 bunch (about 12 stalks) of asparagus	1 tablespoon Japanese soy sauce
salt	toasted white sesame seeds
1 egg yolk	

WASH ASPARAGUS and cut off tough base of stems.

■ Bring a saucepan of lightly salted water to a boil. Slide the hard stalks of the asparagus but not the tender tips, into the water. Return to a boil and simmer until the hard stalks are only just done (*al dente*). Submerge the tips and simmer for 1 minute, or until just tender. Drain and cut into 1-inch pieces.

■ In a bowl, beat the egg yolk until creamy. Blend in the soy sauce and mix well.

■ Arrange asparagus in 4 small bowls. Just before serving, drizzle over the egg sauce and sprinkle over the sesame seeds.

BUROKKORI NO GOMA SHOYU KAKE
■ BROCCOLI WITH SESAME SEEDS ■

SERVES 4

BROCCOLI AND sesame seeds seem made for each other and this simple, tasty vegetable dish is frequently served at Japanese meals. Try it on children who won't eat their greens.

2 3/4 cups small broccoli florets	1 tablespoon Japanese soy sauce
1 1/2 tablespoons water	2 tablespoons toasted sesame seeds

BRING SOME lightly salted water to a boil. Add broccoli and return to a boil. Simmer for 3–4 minutes, or until only just done (*al dente*). Drain well.

■ Mix water, soy sauce and sesame seeds together in a bowl. Toss the broccoli in the dressing. Arrange in 4 small bowls and serve immediately.

INGENMAME NO GOMA SHOYU KAKE
■ GREEN BEANS WITH SESAME ■

SERVES 4

VARIOUS VEGETABLES are frequently cooked in this simple manner in Japan. You can briefly cook almost any other bite-sized pieces of fresh vegetables then, before serving, lightly sprinkle with soy sauce and a scattering of toasted sesame seeds.

■
1/2 pound green beans
salt
■

■
2 tablespoons toasted sesame seeds
Japanese soy sauce
■

WASH AND trim the beans and cut into 3 or 4 pieces.

■ Bring some lightly salted water to a boil in a saucepan. Add beans and return to a boil. Simmer for 2 minutes, or until only just done (*al dente*). Drain.

■ Divide beans among 4 small bowls and sprinkle over the sesame seeds. Just before serving drizzle over a little soy sauce.

HORENSO NO OHITASHI
▪ SPINACH ROLLS WITH SESAME SEEDS ▪

SERVES 4

THIS DISH is very frequently served in Japan. The cooked spinach is formed into a cylinder and sliced into discs. It can be an unexpectedly pleasant revelation for spinach haters and is always a joy for spinach devotees.

1 pound fresh leaf spinach
salt

3 tablespoons toasted sesame seeds
Japanese soy sauce

WASH THE spinach leaves well under running water, removing any damaged parts. Lay the leaves together in a bundle and tie the stems together with cotton thread, or elastic bands. Lower the spinach into a saucepan of lightly salted boiling water, return to a boil and simmer for about 2 minutes.

▪ Remove spinach, plunge into cold water, then drain. Remove the cotton thread, and fold spinach bundle in half. Keeping the bundle together, squeeze excess water out of the spinach either by hand or in a *makisu,* Japanese rolling mat (see page 63) while at the same time forming it into a neat cylinder. With a sharp knife, cut the cylinder into 8 discs.

▪ Divide the spinach discs neatly among 4 small dishes and sprinkle sesame seeds over the top. Just before serving, drizzle over a little soy sauce. This dish is eaten cold.

SATSUMA-IMO SU-AGE
▪ DEEP-FRIED SWEET POTATOES ▪

SERVES 4

Hot, sweet potatoes are sold in Japan in a way rather similar to our roasted chestnuts. Street vendors pull wooden carts containing whole sweet potatoes cooking in small, heated stones, through city streets and housing estates. Nowadays their cart can be a van, and their impressively melodic call of "ishi yaki imo," meaning "stone baked potatoes," often comes from a tape recorder and loud speaker rather than the lungs of the vendor. You can cook sweet potatoes this way by baking them whole in a hot oven, or over a barbecue, or you can make them into this dish, which is an appetizing cross between roasted chestnuts and chips.

■
2 sweet potatoes
vegetable oil for deep-frying
salt

■
schichimi-togarashi (Japanese
seven-spice pepper)

■　　　　　　　　　　　■

PEEL THE sweet potatoes and slice into 1/4-inch-thick slices.

■ Heat oil to 325°F in a saucepan. Deep-fry the potatoes until crisp and golden-brown, taking care not to burn them. Drain on absorbent paper towels.

■ Arrange in 4 small serving bowls or dishes. Sprinkle over a little salt and *schichimi-togarashi*. Serve immediately.

NINJIN NO SHOYU AGE
■ RICE WINE AND SESAME-FRIED CARROTS ■

SERVES 4

TRY THIS way of cooking the humble carrot for a change. Sweet rice wine intensifies the sweetness of carrots and sesame oil adds richness of flavor.

■
1/2 pound carrots 3-4 carrots
1 tablespoon Japanese soy sauce
1 tablespoon *mirin* (sweet rice wine)

■
1 teaspoon superfine sugar
sesame oil
toasted sesame seeds (optional)

■　　　　　　　　　　　■

PEEL THE carrots and cut into matchsticks.

■ Mix soy sauce, *mirin* and sugar, stirring until the sugar has dissolved.

■ Heat a little sesame oil in a frying pan. Add carrots and stir-fry for 2 minutes. Add *mirin* mixture and stir fry over a moderate heat until the liquid has almost all evaporated.

■ Divide among 4 small dishes. Drizzle over a little sesame oil and sprinkle over a few sesame seeds.

OKONOMI YAKI
■ VEGETABLE PANCAKE ■

SERVES 4

IT'S ALWAYS enjoyable to visit one of the many *okonomi yaki* restaurants in Japan where, after selecting your fillings, you cook it all yourself at the table, topping the finished pancake with as much sauce and powdered seaweed as you like.

Okonomi yaki is another example of the Japanese fusing ingredients from other lands with their own and making of it something uniquely Japanese. It is a cross between a thick pancake and a pizza, stuffed with eggs, vegetables and a little pickled ginger and topped with brown sauce, mayonnaise and powdered seaweed—an unlikely sounding yet absolutely delicious combination, and very popular in Japan.

Okonomi yaki makes a delicious light meal on its own, or serve it with soup.

■
2 1/4 cups finely shredded
   green cabbage
1 carrot
1 cup white flour
2 good pinches of sugar
salt
■

■
2/3 cups cold water
1 egg
1 ounce *hajikami shoga*
   (threads of red pickled ginger)
vegetable oil for frying
■

TOPPINGS

■
Japanese *tonkatsu* sauce or English
   brown sauce (such as H.P.)
■

■
Japanese or Hellman's mayonnaise
aonori-ko (powdered seaweed)
■

MIX FLOUR, sugar and salt together in a bowl. Add water and mix well into a batter.

■ Beat the egg in a bowl. Add cabbage, carrot and ginger pickle and mix well. Add to the batter and mix well.

■ Heat about 1 tablespoon oil in a frying pan. Spoon the pancake mixture into the pan, spreading it out into a circle with the back of a spoon. Reduce heat to low to moderate and cover the pan. Fry for about 10 minutes, until the base is golden brown. Turn over the pancake, and fry with the lid off for another 5-6 minutes. While cooking, cut into the top of the pancake in a few places with a knife to allow the steam to escape. Remove from pan onto a warmed plate. Serve with the toppings.

■ To eat, spread about 2-3 tablespoons brown sauce over the pancake, then a similar amount of mayonnaise, and finally sprinkle liberally with powdered seaweed.

ⓥ YASAI NO TEMPURA
■ DEEP-FRIED VEGETABLES IN A LIGHT CRISPY BATTER ■

SERVES 4

TEMPURA IS one of the most popular foods in Japan, and is considered a special treat. It consists of a selection of very fresh vegetables which are cut into bite-sized pieces, dipped into a batter (the only one I know that *should* be lumpy) and briefly deep-fried in vegetable oil until feather-light, golden and crisp, the uneven lumps producing a delicate lacy effect. Before eating, each bitesized morsel is dipped into a delicious sauce, then popped into the mouth for an explosion of flavorful lusciousness.

■ For many years good-quality refined vegetable oil, essential for *tempura*, was difficult to come by for the average person, and *tempura* was mainly eaten at specialty *tempura* restaurants, which gave the dish rarity value and glamour. Now that cooking oil has become available in every Japanese supermarket, cooking *tempura* at home has become commonplace. But no matter how often it appears on the table, the enjoyment of eating these light and lacy golden fritters never wanes, and *tempura* always manages to retain its aura of being a very special treat.

■ You can use safflower, sunflower or rape-seed oil for deep-frying the battered vegetables, but do use new oil if possible.

■ *Tempura* is easy to make. The addition of a bowl of *miso* soup, plain white rice and a selection of crunchy Japanese pickles transforms this delicacy into a minor feast.

■ *Tempura* is usually served with a dipping sauce, and you can either make your own (see page 121) or buy it ready made. I always use the Yamasa brand *tempura* dipping sauce, as it is extremely good and doesn't contain any animal products.

FOR FRYING AND SERVING

tempura dipping sauce
   (see recipe opposite)
or
10.6 fluid ounce bottle of Yamasa
   brand *tempura-tsuyu*
   (dipping sauce)

6 tablespoons grated fresh *daikon*
   (giant white radish), optional
3 spring onions
grated fresh *wasabi* or *wasabi* paste
   (Japanese horseradish)
safflower, sunflower or rape seed oil
   for deep-frying

BATTER

3/4 cup white flour
good pinch of salt

2 egg yolks
3/4 cup iced water

SELECT 4-6 OF THE FOLLOWING VEGETABLES

8 medium cup mushrooms,
   cut in quarters (or 16 button
   mushrooms left whole)
1 carrot, peeled, cut in half, then into
   thin slices, lengthwise
8 fresh baby corn
2 medium onions, peeled and
   cut into 3-4 slices
1 eggplant, cut into quarters lengthwise
   then into bite-sized pieces
1/2 cup green beans,
   trimmed and cut in half

2 green peppers, cut in quarters
   lengthwise,
2/3 cup squash or pumpkin, peeled
   and cut into bite-sized pieces
2 medium-sized Irish potatoes
   or sweet potatoes peeled and cut
   into bite-sized pieces
1 small fresh lotus root, peeled
   and cut into 4-inch slices
1 sheet of *nori* seaweed, cut in half
then into /2-inches strips

FIRST MAKE the *tempura* dipping sauce according to the recipe opposite and keep warm. If using storebought Yamasa *tempura* dipping sauce, put it into a small saucepan, bring to just below the boil and keep warm. It doesn't need to be served very hot.

- Leave the grated *daikon* to drain on absorbent paper towels. Do not squeeze.
- Remove roots and any damaged parts from the spring onions. Wash well and shred very finely, on the diagonal.
- Heat the oil for deep-frying to 350°F.
- Next prepare the batter. Sift the flour with the salt. Lightly beat the egg yolks into the iced water, then stir into the flour to make a batter. Do not overmix—some small lumps and even dry unmixed blobs of flour on the surface are desirable.
- Dip your chosen vegetables in the batter and fry 4 or 5 pieces at a time in the hot oil until crisp and golden. Remove from oil and drain on absorbent paper towels.
- Neatly pile the spring onions, a small cone-shaped mound of grated *daikon* and a little grated *wasabi* onto 4 small dishes. If using a tube of *wasabi* paste, squeeze out about 1-inch per serving.
- Arrange the hot *tempura* on woven bamboo or other plates, lined with *tempura shikishi* or an absorbent white paper napkin.
- Serve immediately, while the *tempura* is still hot and crisp, with individual small bowls of dipping sauce and separate individual small dishes containing a mixture of grated *wasabi*, grated *daikon* and shredded spring onion.
- To eat, mix the *wasabi* and *daikon* into the dipping sauce and sprinkle over the spring onions. Take a piece of *tempura* in chopsticks and dip it into the dipping sauce before popping it into your mouth.

TEMPURA TSUYU
■ TEMPURA DIPPING SAUCE ■

SERVES 4

ALTHOUGH YOU can buy this ready made, it is in fact very simple and quick to prepare yourself. Serve warm not hot.

6 tablespoons *dashi* (see page 30)
2 tablespoons *mirin* (sweet rice wine)

2 tablespoons *sake* (fortified rice wine)
2 tablespoons Japanese soy sauce

PUT ALL the ingredients into a small saucepan and heat to boiling point. Remove from heat and keep warm.

NINJIN NO NORIMAKI
▪ CARROT STICK BUNDLES TIED
WITH SEAWEED ▪

SERVES 4

IN JAPAN the presentation of food is of the utmost importance. Here colorful orange bundles of carrot matchsticks are bound with strips of seaweed.

▪

nori seaweed sheet
1/2 pound carrots (3–4 carrots)
1 tablespoon Japanese soy sauce

▪

▪

1 tablespoon *mirin* (sweet rice wine)
1 teaspoon superfine sugar
sesame oil

▪

CUT EIGHT 1/2-inch wide strips from the sheet of *nori* seaweed.

▪ Peel the carrots and cut into matchsticks of equal length (about 2 1/2-inch long).

▪ Mix soy sauce, *mirin* and sugar, stirring until the sugar has dissolved.

▪ Heat a little sesame oil in a frying pan. Add carrots and stir-fry for 2 minutes. Add *mirin* mixture and stir-fry over a moderate heat until the liquid has almost all evaporated.

▪ Arranging the carrot sticks neatly side by side, divide them into 8 equal portions. Wind a strip of *nori* seaweed around the center of each portion to form a tied bundle.

▪ Divide the carrot bundles among 4 small dishes and drizzle over a little sesame oil.

NIRANEGI NO GOMA YAKI

■ SESAME-GRILLED LEEKS ■

SERVES 4

JAPANESE LEEKS are smaller, sweeter and more tender than Western leeks so try to select young, slender leeks for this dish. Grilling the young leeks brings out their flavor, and the dark sesame oil adds richness.

6–8 leeks
2 tablespoons sesame oil
3 tablespoons Japanese soy sauce

schichimi-togarashi (Japanese seven-spice pepper)

CUT OFF the hard root part and tough outer leaves of the leeks. Cut in half lengthwise, three quarters of the way through into the white part. Wash well under a running tap, opening out the leaves to remove any grit. Cut into 1 1/2-inch pieces.

■ Mix together the sesame oil and soy sauce in a bowl large enough to hold the leeks. Toss the leeks in the mixture and marinate for 10 minutes. Drain, then spread out on a baking sheet or piece of foil. Heat under a medium broil, or over a barbecue, turning from time to time until just tender and just turning brown. Serve with *schichimi-togarashi* to sprinkle over.

ODEN
■ SIMMERED VEGETABLES
SOY BEAN CURD AND EGG ■

SERVES 4

PRESSED FOR space, Japan's larger cities are continuously building both higher and deeper. In Tokyo and Osaka, Japan's second largest city, there are high-rise blocks composed entirely of specialty restaurants, one to a floor, while 40 feet below the cities lie a subterranean complex of intercommunicating "towns" each with its own unique coordinated style, and with individual names such as "White City" and "Rainbow City." They are light, bright places fresh with air-conditioning, fountains and trees. Here you can find street upon street of retail shops, restaurants and the basements of the department stores above. Some streets are lined on either side entirely with restaurants, some plushily modern and others mirroring "old Japan." In one of the latter, designed inside and out to resemble an old Japanese farmhouse, and looking rather incongruous in the center of a glitteringly modern subterranean city, I occasionally enjoyed a steaming bowl of *oden* served with searingly hot Japanese mustard— a traditional country dish, and very welcome on a bitter Japanese winter day.

Vegans may omit the eggs.

■

10 ounces fresh *tofu* (soy bean curd)
8 ounces *konnyaku*, optional
8 ounces *daikon* (giant white radish)
6 sheets of *aburage* (flat, fried soy
    bean curd)
6 outer leaves of Chinese cabbage
2 medium-sized potatoes
2 carrots

■

■

vegetable oil for deep-frying
6 cups *dashi* (see page 30)
2 tablespoons Japanese soy sauce
2 tablespoons *mirin* (sweet rice wine)
1 tablespoon superfine sugar
6 shelled hard-boiled eggs, optional
salt
Japanese or English mustard

■

WRAP THE *tofu* in a clean kitchen towel and leave for 30 minutes to drain off excess water. Cut into 4 squares, then cut each square in half, on the diagonal, to form 8 triangles in all.

■ Cut the *konnyaku* into similar triangles.

■ Peel and cut the *daikon* into 1-inch rounds or squares, beveling off the sharp edges with a knife. Cut a star into the top of each piece. This helps them keep their shape while cooking. (See illustration on following page.)

- Pour boiling water over *aburage*, to remove excess oil, and drain. Cut into 1-inch squares.
- Wash the cabbage leaves and cut into 1-inch strips.
- Peel the potatoes and cut into quarters.
- Peel the carrots and cut into 1/2-inch rounds.
- In a large saucepan, heat the oil to 350°F. Deep-fry the *tofu* triangles until they are golden and crisp on the outside. Drain on absorbent paper towels.
- Put *dashi*, soy sauce, *mirin* and sugar into a large saucepan and bring to a boil. Add *daikon* and carrot, return to a boil and simmer until almost tender. Add *tofu*, *aburage*, *konnyaku*, hard-boiled eggs, potatoes and cabbage leaves. Return to a boil and simmer for about 20 minutes, or until the potatoes are done but not overdone. Add salt to taste.
- Divide among 4 large bowls and serve with mustard.

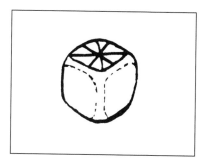

HARUMAKI
▪ JAPANESE-STYLE VEGETABLE
SPRING ROLLS ▪

MAKES 16 SPRING ROLLS TO SERVE 4-5

SPRING ROLLS originated in China, but this Japanese version is my favorite. They can be eaten as a snack, or as a light meal with plain rice and a Japanese salad.

▪

6 dried *shiitake* mushrooms
1 1/2-inch piece of fresh ginger root
6 sheets of *aburage*
    (flat, fried soy bean curd)
Japanese soy sauce
3 tablespoons *sake* (fortified rice wine)
1 carrot
3 spring onions

▪

▪

2 tablespoons sesame oil
salt
1 3/4 cups fresh bean sprouts
1 tablespoon flour
vegetable oil for deep-frying
16 spring roll skins
    (or Chinese *wonton* skins)

▪

SOAK THE *shiitake* mushrooms in warm water for 30 minutes. A small plate or saucer on the mushrooms will keep them submerged. Drain. Remove hard stems, then squeeze the mushroom caps to remove excess water. Cut into thin slices.

▪ Meanwhile, remove any discolored parts from the ginger and coarsely grate.

▪ Cut *aburage* in half lengthwise, then cut into thin strips widthwise.

▪ In a bowl, mix together 2 tablespoons soy sauce and 2 tablespoons *sake*. Add *aburage* and stir to coat. Leave to marinate for 10 minutes, then drain.

▪ Peel carrot and shred on a coarse grater.

▪ Trim roots and any damaged leaves from the spring onions. Wash and finely shred, on the diagonal.

▪ Wash and pat-dry the bean sprouts.

▪ Heat the sesame oil in a saucepan. Add ginger and carrot and stir-fry for 2 minutes. Add mushrooms and 2/3 of the spring onions (reserving the remainder for garnish), and stir-fry for 1 minute. Add 1 tablespoon soy sauce, 1 tablespoon *sake* and salt to taste. Add the *aburage* and stir-fry for another minute.

▪ Remove from heat. Add bean sprouts and stir. Divide into 16 portions and leave to cool.

▪ Mix the flour into a stiff paste with a little water.

- Preheat the vegetable oil in a large saucepan to 350°F.
- Lay a spring roll skin out flat. Place 1 oblong-shaped portion of the filling across the spring roll, just below the center.
- Take the lower corner and fold it over the filling.
- Repeat with left and right corners.
- Dab a little flour and water paste on the fourth corner.
- Roll up tightly away from you. Press the pasted corner to secure. Repeat with remaining ingredients.

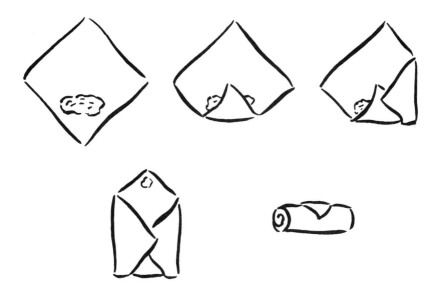

- Cook the spring rolls as soon as possible. If they are left standing around the skins can gradually absorb moisture and soften, making them fragile and easy to tear.
- Drop 4 spring rolls at a time into the hot oil, moving them around in the oil until they are crisp and golden-brown. Drain on absorbent paper towels and keep hot.
- Divide spring rolls among 4 small plates. Sprinkle over remaining spring onion and serve with soy sauce to drizzle over. Eat piping hot.

KONNYAKU NO YASAI NI

■ KONNYAKU SIMMERED WITH VEGETABLES ■

SERVES 4

KONNYAKU IS a helpful aid to slimming as it is said to be calorie-free. It is processed from the root of the *Amorphallus konjac* (devil's tongue) and is eaten in Japan to help clear the digestive tract.

■

6 dried *shiitake* mushrooms
1 carrot
8 ounces *konnyaku*

■

2 tablespoons Japanese soy sauce
2 tablespoons *sake* (fortified rice wine)
2 teaspoons *mirin* (sweet rice wine)

SOAK THE mushrooms in warm water for 30 minutes. A small plate or saucer will keep them submerged. Drain mushrooms, reserving soaking water. Remove stems and discard. Squeeze the mushroom caps a little to remove excess water. Cut mushroom caps in half.

■ Meanwhile, peel carrot and cut into slices about 1/2-inch thick. Shape into cherry blossoms (optional—see page 17).

■ Cut *konnyaku* into 1/2-inch x 2-inches slices. Bring some unsalted water to a boil in a saucepan. Add *konnyaku*. Return to a boil and simmer for 2-3 minutes. Drain.

■ Heat a dry frying pan and dry-fry the *konnyaku* over a moderate heat, turning, for 2 minutes to remove excess water.

■ Into a saucepan put 1 cup mushroom soaking water (top up with water if necessary). Add soy sauce, *sake* and *mirin* and bring to a boil. Add *konnyaku*, mushrooms and carrots. Return to a boil and simmer for 10 minutes. Drain.

■ Arrange *konnyaku*, mushrooms and carrots on 4 small dishes and serve immediately.

EGG DISHES

Raw eggs are rather more appreciated in Japan than in the West, and raw egg curry is one of several curry dishes served with truly astonishing speed at the many popular curry bars. Amazingly, your portion of rice has been heaped onto a dish before you've shut the door, and even as you order at the serving bar, a thick and fragrant Japanese curry sauce is simultaneously ladled over the rice then topped with, say, a raw egg and pickled vegetable. As you reach your table your raw egg curry and complimentary bowl of green tea usually arrive before you've sat down.

If you wish to make raw egg or any other Japanese curry, solidified Japanese curry roux, which looks like a bar of milk chocolate, is available at most Japanese food shops and many supermarkets in this country. Simply melt it into boiling water and within seconds you have a delectable Japanese curry sauce to pour over vegetables, or whatever else you fancy. If you have the courage, you can even crack a raw egg over it! Raw eggs are also cracked into hot miso soup, hot rice, or beaten into a variety of drinks and tossed down as a pick-me-up.

Eggs are also cooked into various delectable dishes such as light and silky savory egg custard; beaten and gently cooked with tofu, seaweed or onions; or made into thick rolled omelets and cut into discs.

Tiny flecked and spotted quails' eggs are also available everywhere in Japan and are delicious cracked open and dropped into clear soups.

MUSHI TAMAGO
■ STEAMED EGGS AND ONION
WITH SEAWEED GARNISH ■

SERVES 4

A VERY quickly made dish of gently cooked eggs enlivened with spring onions and seaweed. Simple, but one of my favorites.

■
4 spring onions
4 packetsof *ajitsuke-nori* seaweed
8 eggs
■

■
1 cup water
4 tablespoons Japanese soy sauce
■

REMOVE ROOTS and any damaged leaves from the spring onions. Wash well and shred finely, on the diagonal.

■ Using scissors, cut the *ajitsuke-nori* seaweed into fine strips, lengthwise.

■ Beat the eggs. Add water, soy sauce and spring onions and stir. Pour into a saucepan. Cover with a lid and cook very gently over a low heat until the eggs are only just set. *Do not overcook the eggs.*

■ Divide the eggs among 4 small bowls. Sprinkle over the shredded *nori* seaweed and serve immediately.

NORI TAMADOFU
■ EGGS AND SOY BEAN CURD WITH SEAWEED GARNISH ■

SERVES 4

THIS DISH of lightly cooked eggs and *tofu* is very popular in Japan.

about 10 ounces fresh tofu
   (soy bean curd)
4 packets of ajitsuke-nori seaweed

6 tablespoons Japanese soy sauce
4 teaspoons mirin (sweet rice wine)
4 eggs

WRAP THE *tofu* in a clean kitchen towel and leave for 30 minutes to drain excess water. Cut into 1-inch cubes.

■ With scissors, cut the *ajitsuke-nori* seaweed into fine strips, lengthwise.

■ Put the soy sauce and *mirin* in a saucepan and bring to a boil. Carefully add the *tofu*. Cover with a lid and simmer gently on a low heat for 4-5 minutes.

■ In the meantime, beat the eggs and pour over the *tofu*. Replace the lid and continue to cook over a low heat until the eggs are only just set. *Do not overcook the eggs.*

■ Divide among 4 small bowls. Sprinkle over the shredded *nori* seaweed and serve immediately.

ⓥ NORI TAMAGO YAKI
■ SEAWEED EGG ROLLS ■

SERVES 4

JAPANESE OMELETS are usually rolled up and sliced into discs. Ideally you need a small, rectangular Japanese frying pan, *tamago yoki nabe*. However you can use an ordinary frying pan (see variation, below).

■

5 eggs
1 1/2 tablespoons Japanese soy sauce
1 tablespoon *mirin* (sweet rice wine)

■

vegetable oil for frying
8 packets of *ajitsuke-nori* seaweed
toasted sesame seeds

■

BEAT THE eggs. Blend in soy sauce and *mirin*.

■ Oil a Japanese straight-sided omelet pan, and heat. Pour in 1/8 (about an egg cup full) of the beaten eggs. Tilt to coat the pan. Crush one packet of *nori* over the omelet. When the egg has nearly set, roll the farthest part towards you, using chopsticks or a spatula, to form a cylinder. Push the cylinder to the back of the pan and pour in another 1/8 of the beaten egg. Lift the cylinder so that the egg mixture runs underneath it. Crush another packet of *nori* over the omelet. When the second omelet has nearly set, roll the egg cylinder towards you causing the second omelet to wrap around it to make a thicker cylinder. Push the cylinder to the back of the pan and continue as above with remaining egg and *nori* to produce one thick rolled omelet, oiling the pan as necessary.

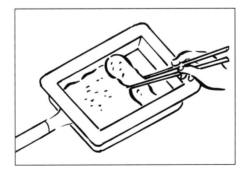

■ Spread out a *makisu* (Japanese rolling mat), smooth side uppermost with the bamboo strips running from left to right. Lay the egg roll on the mat widthwise. Lift the egg roll in the mat and roll it away from you while pressing the mat firmly around the omelet to shape it into a neat, firm cylinder (see illustration below). Leave egg roll to settle for about 10 minutes. With a sharp knife, cut into 8 discs.

■ Arrange the omelet discs attractively on 4 small dishes and sprinkle over a few sesame seeds. Serve with soy sauce to drizzle over. This dish is usually eaten cold.

VARIATION

If you don't have a Japanese omelet pan and rolling mat, make a Western-style omelet with all the omelet mixture. When nearly done, crush all the *ajitsuke-nori* evenly over the top and roll it up like a jelly roll as firmly as you can. Transfer to a plate and leave to settle for 10 minutes. Cut into discs and serve as above.

ⓥ NEGI TAMAGO YAKI
▪ROLLED ONION OMELET▪

SERVES 4

THIS CLASSIC Japanese omelet is usually served as part of a lunch box, *bento*, and is eaten cold.

5 spring onions
5 eggs
1 1/2 tablespoons Japanese soy sauce

1 tablespoon *mirin* (sweet rice wine)
vegetable oil for frying

TRIM ROOTS and any damaged leaves from the spring onions. Wash well and finely shred, on the diagonal.

▪ Beat the eggs. Blend in soy sauce and stir in the spring onions.

▪ Oil a Japanese straight-sided omelet pan, *tamago yoki nabe*, and heat. Pour in 1/8 (about an egg cup full) of the beaten eggs. Tilt to coat the pan. When the egg has almost set, roll the farthest part towards you to form a cylinder using chopsticks or a spatula. Push the cylinder to the back of the pan and pour in another 1/8 of the beaten egg. Lift the cylinder so that the egg mixture runs underneath it. When the second omelet has almost set, roll the cylinder towards you, causing the second omelet to wrap around it making one thicker cylinder. Continue as above with remaining egg mixture to produce one thick rolled omelet, oiling the pan as necessary (see illustration in previous recipe).

▪ Spread out a *makisu* (Japanese rolling mat), smooth side upper-most with the bamboo strips running from left to right. Lay the egg roll on the mat widthwise. Lift the egg roll in the mat and roll it away from you while pressing the mat firmly around the omelet to shape it into a neat, firm cylinder (see illustration for previous recipe). Leave egg roll to settle for about 10 minutes. With a sharp knife, cut into 8 discs.

Arrange the omelet discs attractively on 4 small dishes. Serve with soy sauce to drizzle over.

VARIATION

If you don't have a Japanese omelet pan and rolling mat, make a Western-style omelet with the omelet and onion mixture. When nearly done, roll it up like a jelly roll as firmly as you can. Transfer to a plate and leave to settle for 10 minutes. With a sharp knife cut it into discs and serve as above.

SAVORY EGG CUSTARDS

TAMAGO DOFU
■ STEAMED EGG *TOFU* ■

SERVES

THIS LIGHT yet sustaining dish can be served at any meal, and is ideal to tempt the jaded appetite of an invalid. *Tamago* "dofu" (or "*tofu*") is named after the fragile silken *tofu* which it resembles.

4 eggs
1 1/2 cups cold *dashi* (see page 30)
2 teaspoons *mirin* (sweet rice wine)

1/2 teaspoon salt
mustard greens and watercress,
    optional

S E A S O N I N G   S A U C E

1/2 cups *dashi* (see page 30)
4 teaspoons Japanese soy sauce

2 teaspoons *mirin* (sweet rice wine)

SMOOTHLY LINE a 1-pound loaf tin with 2 layers of foil.

■ Lightly beat the eggs in a bowl without forming froth. Blend in *dashi, mirin* and salt. Pour the egg mixture into the loaf tin through a fine strainer or cheesecloth. Remove any bubbles with a teaspoon. Heat some water to boiling point in a steamer. Put in the loaf tin. Put the lid on with a clean kitchen towel underneath it. Gently cook on a low heat for about 30 minutes, or until the egg custard is completely set. (Too high a heat can cause the egg custard to curdle.) Place a few strands of mustard and watercress on top of the custard and steam for another 10 seconds. To test for setting, press custard lightly in the center: if it feels firm and springs back, it is set.

■ Remove loaf tin from the steamer and leave to cool. Gently lift out the egg *tofu* in the foil. Carefully remove egg *tofu* from the foil onto a plate. With a sharp knife, cut in half lengthwise, then cut across 3 times to make 8 cubes. Carefully divide among 4 small dishes.

■ Put sauce ingredients into a saucepan and bring to a boil. Simmer for 1 minute, then pour over the egg *tofu*. Dab a little *wasabi* paste on the side of each dish. This dish is eaten cold.

CHAWAN MUSHI
▪ STEAMED SAVORY
VEGETABLE CUSTARD ▪

SERVES 4

AN EXQUISITE delicacy of eggs and vegetables laced with *mirin* and *sake*. Although set, it retains some liquid which seeps from the vegetables, causing it to be regarded almost as a soup.

▪

3 dried *shiitake* mushrooms
4 asparagus tips
salt
1 spring onion
1 carrot
2 tablespoons Japanese soy sauce

▪

1 tablespoon *mirin* (sweet rice wine)
3 tablespoons *sake* (fortified rice wine)
4 eggs
mustard greens and watercress,
   optional

▪

SOAK THE *shiitake* mushrooms in 2 cups warm water for 30 minutes. Remove mushrooms, reserving the soaking water. Remove the hard stalks and discard. Lightly squeeze the mushroom caps to remove excess liquid. With scissors, cut into fine strips.

▪ Wash asparagus tips. Boil for 2 minutes in lightly salted water, then drain.

▪ Remove roots and any damaged leaves from the spring onion. Wash well, then shred finely, on the diagonal.

▪ Peel the carrot and cut into fine matchsticks.

▪ Put reserved mushroom soaking water, soy sauce, *mirin* and into a saucepan and bring to a boil. Add mushrooms and carrot. Return to a boil and simmer for 2 minutes. Salt to taste. Drain, reserving the cooking stock. If necessary, make the stock up to 2 cups with water and leave to cool.

▪ Lightly beat the eggs without forming froth, then blend into the cooled stock. Strain through a fine strainer. Remove any bubbles.

▪ Arrange the asparagus tips, mushroom and carrot in the bottom of 4 *chawan mushi* cups or deep mugs. Pour in the egg mixture until the cups are about 4/5 full. Remove any bubbles with a teaspoon, then sprinkle the spring onion on top.

▪ Heat some water in a steamer to boiling point. Place the cups inside. Cover with a lid with a kitchen towel underneath it. Gently cook on a low heat for about 20-25 minutes, or until set. (Too high a heat can cause the egg custard to curdle.) Place a few strands of mustard and watercress on top of each custard and steam for another 10 seconds. Press custard lightly in the center: if it feels firm and springs back, it is set. Serve hot in the mugs and eat with a spoon.

JAPANESE-STYLE SALADS

S alads flourish all the year round at the edge of my parents-in-law's paddy field. The little plot was, until recently, tended every day by Hannae, my father-in-law's aunt, until she was well into her nineties. Her tiny, frail figure, clad in a simple kimono, was frequently seen bending over to weed or pick the various salads that brought a ray of sunshine to winter meals or bestowed refreshment in the humid Japanese summer.

Urban Japanese housewives make daily excursions to shops and supermarkets to purchase flawless, exquisitely fresh produce from a dazzling array of fruits, vegetables, fungi and salads, all scrupulously cleaned and carefully set out like exotic prize-winning displays. There's not a limp leaf or blemish to be seen because the Japanese, like the French, demand and get the most superlative quality and freshness.

Edible flowers such as violets, squash blossoms, primroses, mimosa, cherry, plum and apple blossoms, chive flowers, pansies, marigolds, rose petals and nasturtiums provide the most charming garnishes for Japanese salads.

KYURI NO WAKAME AE
■ SEAWEED AND CUCUMBER SALAD ■

SERVES 4

A VERY popular salad, cool and refreshing with a tangy, sharp, sweet dressing.

■
1 length or 1/4-ounce packet of
  dried *wakame* seaweed
1 cucumber
3 tablespoons *su*
  (Japanese rice vinegar)

■
1 1/2 tablespoons superfine sugar
1 tablespoon Japanese soy sauce
toasted sesame seeds
salt

■

SOAK THE *wakame* from the packet in warm water for 20 minutes, or until expanded and soft, then drain. If using a length of *wakame*, after soaking as above remove the hard edge and discard, then cut remaining length of *wakame* into 1/2-inch bite-sized pieces.
■ Peel the cucumber. Cut in half lengthwise, then slice crosswise into paper-thin slices.
■ Mix vinegar, sugar and soy sauce together. Add salt to taste.
■ Toss cucumber and *wakame* together and pile neatly into 4 small bowls. Top with dressing and sprinkle over a few sesame seeds.

KYURI NO MISO AE
■ CUCUMBER WITH
SOY BEAN PASTE DRESSING ■

SERVES 4

A SIMPLE tasty salad of cucumber half-moons in a *miso* dressing.

■
1 cucumber
5 tablespoons *aka miso*
  (red soy bean paste)

■
2 tablespoons *mirin* (sweet rice wine)
salt

■

WASH THE cucumber. Cut in half lengthwise, then slice thinly, crosswise.
■ Mix the aka *miso* and *mirin* together. Add salt to taste.
■ Neatly pile the cucumber into 4 small bowls and top with *miso* dressing.

MOYASHI NO WASABI AE

■ BEAN SPROUT AND CUCUMBER SALAD WITH JAPANESE HORSERADISH DRESSING ■

SERVES 4

ULTRA CRISPNESS laced with the zap of Japanese horseradish.

■

2 1/4 cups fresh bean sprouts
1/2 cucumber
4 tablespoons *su* (Japanese rice vinegar)
1 tablespoon Japanese soy sauce

■

1/2 tablespoon superfine sugar
1/2 teaspoon *wasabi* paste
(Japanese horseradish paste)
good pinch of salt

■

WASH THE bean sprouts to remove the husks, then shake dry. Wash the cucumber. Cut in half lengthwise, then slice finely crosswise.
■ Toss the cucumber and bean sprouts together and pile neatly into 4 small bowls.
■ Mix vinegar, soy sauce, sugar, *wasabi* paste and salt together and pour over the salad.

Geese—see over there.
A field of nice greens
For you.

ISSA (1763-1827)

DAIKON NAMASU
■ CHILLED GIANT RADISH AND CARROT SALAD ■

SERVES 4

FIELDS FULL of green, feathery leaves of the giant radish, *daikon*, are a common sight in the Japanese countryside, and their crisp, white roots combine well with carrots.

■
4 tablespoons *su* (Japanese rice vinegar)
1/2 tablespoon superfine sugar
1 tablespoon Japanese soy sauce
■

■
10 ounces *daikon* (giant white radish)
3 carrots
salt
■

MIX VINEGAR, sugar and soy sauce together in a small bowl, then refrigerate.
■ Peel the radish and carrots and cut into matchsticks. Spread out on a large dish and sprinkle lightly with salt. Refrigerate for 30 minutes. then pat dry with a clean kitchen towel.
■ Just before serving, neatly pile the vegetables into 4 small bowls or dishes and pour over the dressing.

INGENMANE MISO AE
■ GREEN BEAN SALAD WITH SOY BEAN PASTE DRESSING ■

SERVES 4

RICHLY FLAVORED soy bean paste, *miso*, envelopes the slightly crisp beans. Runner beans may also be used, sliced on the diagonal into 1/2-inch pieces.

■
1 pound green beans
2 tablespoons *aka miso* (red soy bean paste)

■
1 tablespoon *mirin* (sweet rice wine)

Top and tail the beans. Boil in lightly salted water until only just done (*al dente*). Drain and plunge into cold water, then drain again. Slice beans into 3 or 4 pieces, on the diagonal.

- In a bowl, mix *miso* paste and *mirin* into a smooth cream. Toss the beans in the *miso* mixture.
- Divide among 4 small bowls.

ASUPARAGUSU NO KIMIZU
ASPARAGUS SALAD WITH KIMIZU DRESSING

SERVES 4

THE LUXURY of fresh asparagus is here complemented with a smooth, delicately sweet-and-sour dressing to create a delicious salad for a special meal.

1 bunch (about 12 stalks) of asparagus
salt
1 tablespoon *su* (Japanese rice vinegar)

1 tablespoon Custer sugar
1 tablespoon water
1 egg yolk

WASH ASPARAGUS and cut off tough base of stems.

- Bring a saucepan of lightly salted water to a boil. Slide the hard stalks of the asparagus, but not the tender tips, into the water. Simmer the hard stalks for 1 minute before submerging tips. Simmer until tender. Drain and cut into 1-inch pieces and divide among 4 small bowls.
- Mix vinegar, sugar, water and 1 teaspoon salt in a small saucepan and cook over a low heat, stirring, until the sugar has dissolved. Add egg yolk, a little at a time, while stirring. Cook egg mixture in double boiler or over a larger saucepan of boiling water, stirring until thick and creamy. Do not overcook or it will harden. Pour the *kimizu* dressing over the asparagus.

BUROKKORI NO GOMA AE
■ BROCCOLI SALAD WITH SESAME DRESSING ■

SERVES 4

JAPANESE VEGETABLES are very lightly cooked. When the broccoli is cooked it should still be slightly crisp, not soft. Plunging it into cold water stops the cooking process, which would otherwise continue even after you have drained it.

9 ounces small broccoli florets
   (about 3 cups)
salt
3 ounces *daikon* (giant radish),
   optional

4 tablespoons toasted sesame seeds
3 tablespoons Japanese soy sauce
1 tablespoon superfine sugar

Bring some lightly salted water to a boil. Add broccoli and return to a boil. Simmer for 2-3 minutes, or until just done (*al dente*). Drain, plunge the broccoli into cold water, then drain again.
■ Peel the *daikon* and slice into paper-thin slices.
■ Finely crush 3 tablespoons of the sesame seeds in a *suribashi* (Japanese pestle and mortar) or with a rolling pin. Mix with soy sauce, sugar and a pinch of salt.
■ Divide the broccoli among 4 small bowls. Arrange the *daikon* over the top and pour over the sesame dressing. Sprinkle remaining sesame seeds over the top.

RENKON AE
■ LOTUS ROOT AND SWEET RED PEPPER SALAD IN *SAKE* DRESSING ■

SERVES 4

FRESH LOTUS root is often sold in Chinese food shops. Canned lotus root are not suitable for this recipe. The flower-patterned white discs of lotus and the scarlet pepper in a perky *sake* dressing enliven any meal.

■
8 ounces fresh lotus root
1 tablespoon *su* (Japanese rice vinegar)
1/2 cup *sake* (fortified rice wine)
2 tablespoons water
■

■
2 tablespoons superfine sugar
1/2 teaspoon salt
1/2 sweet red pepper
■

PEEL THE lotus root and cut into 1/2-inch slices. Immediately submerge in a pan of cold water to which you have added the vinegar. The lotus slices may be cut into flowers—see page 108.

■ Bring vinegar water and lotus to a boil and simmer for 2–3 minutes until the lotus is tender but still crisp. Drain.

■ Put *sake*, 2 tablespoons water, sugar and salt into a small pan. Bring to a boil, stirring to dissolve the sugar. Drain the lotus slices and put into a bowl. Pour over hot *sake* mixture and leave to marinate for 30 minutes. Drain, reserving the *sake* sauce.

■ Meanwhile, wash the red pepper, then slice into very fine rings, removing seeds and membranes. Alternatively cut into small diamonds.

■ Divide lotus root among 4 small bowls. Pour over a little of the *sake* sauce and decorate with the red pepper.

KYURI NO UMEBOSHI AE
■ CUCUMBER AND WATERCRESS SALAD IN PICKLED PLUM DRESSING ■

SERVES 4

THE REFRESHING crispness of cucumber and cress marries well with this rich plumy dressing.

■
1 cucumber
1 bunch watercress
2 umeboshi (pickled plums)
■

■
1 1/2 tablespoons *mirin* (sweet rice wine)
1 tablespoon Japanese soy sauce
salt
■

PEEL CUCUMBER, cut into matchsticks and drain on a kitchen towel.

■ Wash watercress and shake dry.

■ Remove stones from the *umeboshi* and mash the fruit. Mix with *mirin*, soy sauce and a pinch of salt.

■ Toss the cucumber and cress in the plum dressing and pile onto 4 small individual dishes.

TAKENOKO AE
■ FRESH BAMBOO SHOOT SALAD ■

SERVES 4

THE FRESH bamboo shoots that push through the mountain under-growth in the spring have the fragrant, earthy taste of the Japanese mountains, where they grow wild in great profusion. Where left they ultimately form great forests of bamboo. Canned bamboo shoots are not suitable for this dish.

■

8 ounces fresh bamboo shoots
salt
4 tablespoons *su* (Japanese rice
    vinegar)

■

2 tablespoons *mirin* (sweet rice wine)
1 tablespoon superfine sugar
2 tablespoons *mirin* (sweet rice wine)
schichimi-togarashi (Japanese
    seven-spice pepper)

■   ■

Wash bamboo shoots well. Cover with lightly salted water and bring to a boil. Simmer for 30 minutes, or until tender. Drain and remove skin. Slice into rounds and then into matchsticks.

■ Mix together vinegar, *mirin*, sugar, and good pinch of salt and pour over the bamboo shoots. Leave to marinate for 30 minutes, then drain, reserving the liquid.

■ Divide the bamboo shoots among 4 small bowls. Pour over some of the marinade and sprinkle over a little *schichimi-togarashi*.

HARUSAME TO KYURI NO SUNOMONO
▪ SPRING RAIN NOODLES AND CUCUMBER SALAD ▪

SERVES 4

POETICALLY NAMED spring rain noodles are thin, translucent strands made of potato or soy bean starch. They are sold dried, in packets. Make sure you select the thin salad *harusame*. Ask if you're not sure!

3 ounces dried *harusame* noodles
salt
2-inches piece of cucumber
1 tablespoon *su* (Japanese rice vinegar)

2 teaspoons water or *dashi* (see page 30)
2 teaspoons Japanese soy sauce
2 teaspoons *mirin* (sweet rice wine)
1 teaspoon superfine sugar

BRING A large saucepan of lightly salted water to a boil. Add noodles and return to a boil. Fast boil for 5 minutes. Drain and plunge noodles into cold water, stirring gently to separate the strands, until noodles are cold. Drain and set aside.

▪ Wash the cucumber, cut in half lengthwise, then cut across into paper-thin slices.

▪ Put vinegar, water or *dashi*, soy sauce, *mirin*, sugar and a good pinch of salt into a small bowl. Stir until the sugar has dissolved.

▪ Mix noodles, cucumber and dressing together and chill in the refrigerator. Divide among 4 small bowls.

SHIRATAKI TO KYURI NO SUNOMONO
▪ *SHIRATAKI* NOODLES AND CUCUMBER ▪

SERVES 2-4

SHIRATAKI NOODLES are processed from the root of the "devil's tongue." They are a great help to those on a slimming diet as they are filling, yet have no calories. They are eaten in Japan to help clear the digestive tract of toxins.

Proceed as for previous recipe, substituting *shirataki* noodles for the *harusame*.

JAPANESE
PICKLES

■ **T S U K E   M O N O** ■

For hundreds of years, many types of vegetables and fruits have been pickled in Japanese farmhouses by packing them into huge wooden barrels and covering them in salt, vinegar, rice bran or miso (fermented soy bean paste). Some of the resulting relishes would be donated to the local temples to enliven the diets of the fortunate monks, the remainder were taken to market. Farmhouse pickles can still be found in Japan, but more often commercially produced pickles are bought and served. They are of excellent quality, come in many varieties and are usually sealed in flat plastic packages.

At almost every Japanese meal, including breakfast, pickles are on the table and Japanese plain white rice, which is cooked without salt, is always eaten with a tangy pickle. There are few set rules as to which variety of pickle goes with which dish. It is nice to have 2 or 3 different pickles on the table so everyone can select their favorite.

Many Japanese housewives make their own pickles, and as they are fairly expensive to buy in this country it's worth making some of your own. The following are a few popular traditional Japanese pickles which are very quick and easy to make. For the best results they should be allowed to mature before eating—one for a month, another for 2 days, and a couple overnight. However, if you have forgotten to make, or couldn't obtain, any Japanese pickles to serve with your Japanese meal, I have included two "instant" pickle recipes on page 150.

NINNIKU NO TSUKE MONO

■ GARLIC PICKLES ■

SERVES 4

THESE SWEET and flavorful crispy garlic pickles are a delicacy eaten with plain white rice. My grandmother-in-law, Hatsuko, made garlic pickles every year. She gave me a large bottle of the beautiful, golden cloves, advising me to eat one or two a day for good health— far more enjoyable than garlic capsules.

To make this pickle, select fresh, firm garlic bulbs with average-sized (not too large or too small) cloves.

■

3–4 garlic bulb
1 cup water
2 tablespoons *mirin* (sweet rice wine)

■

2 tablespoons superfine sugar
good pinch of salt
4 tablespoons *aka miso*
    (red soy bean paste)

■

SEPARATE THE garlic cloves and peel.

■ Sterilize a 1-pint canning jar and lid in boiling water and fill with the garlic cloves.

■ Put water, *mirin*, sugar and salt into a saucepan and bring to a boil, stirring.

■ Put the *aka miso* into a bowl and mix into a smooth cream with some of the hot liquid. Stir the creamed *miso* into the remaining liquid, then pour over the garlic cloves to cover. Close the lid tightly and leave in a very cool, dark place, or refrigerate, for 1 month. The pickles are now ready to eat.

■ To store, refrigerate in a lidded container.

HAKUSAI NO TSUKE MONO
▪ SALT-PICKLED CHINESE CABBAGE ▪

SERVES 4

A CRISP and juicy country pickle to awaken a sluggish palate and complement any Japanese meal.

▪

1 head (about 12 ounces)
   of Chinese cabbage

▪

▪

1 1/2 tablespoons salt
Japanese soy sauce

▪

CUT THE hard root end from the cabbage. Separate the leaves and spread them out on a large serving dish or chopping board. Sprinkle the salt over both sides of the leaves. Put another large dish or chopping board on the leaves and place a 2-pound weight, or a saucepan full of water, on top. Leave in a cool place for 2 days.

▪ Plunge the leaves into a bowl of cold water, swish them around, then drain. Cut into 1-inch lengths. Take the leaves in your fist and squeeze out as much water as you can. The pickles are now ready to eat. Before serving, mix with a few drops of soy sauce.

▪ To store, refrigerate in a lidded container.

KYURI NO ICHIYA ZUKE
▪ OVERNIGHT CRISPY SALT-PICKLED CUCUMBER ▪

SERVES 4

THIS FRESH-TASTING, simple pickle is very easy to make and nicely complements plain white rice.

▪

1 cucumber

▪

▪

1 1/2 tablespoons salt

▪

TRIM THE ends and wash the cucumber. Cut in half lengthwise and scoop out the seeds with a teaspoon. Cut each piece in half again lengthwise, then in half crosswise.

■ Spread the cucumber out on a large plate. Sprinkle over the salt, then arrange the cucumber skin side up. Put another plate or chopping board on the cucumber and place a 2-pound weight, or a saucepan full of water, on the top. Leave to marinate overnight.

■ Plunge cucumber into cold water, then drain. Arrange the cucumber pieces side by side in a bundle. Take the bundle in your hands and squeeze out as much water as you can. With scissors, cut into bite-sized pieces about 1/2-inch long. The pickle is now ready to eat. To store, refrigerate in a lidded container.

KYURI TO SHOGA NO ICHIYA ZUKE
■ OVERNIGHT GINGERED CRISPY CUCUMBER PICKLE ■

SERVES 4

THIS PICKLE takes the previous recipe one stage further. After the salted cucumber has been weighted and left overnight, then the water squeezed out of it, it is dressed with grated ginger, soy sauce and Japanese seven-spice pepper (*schichimi-togarashi*).

1 cucumber	2 tablespoons Japanese soy sauce
1 1/2 tablespoons salt	1/2 teaspoon *schichimi-togarashi*
1 ounce fresh ginger root	(Japanese seven-spice pepper)

TRIM THE ends and wash the cucumber. Cut in halves lengthwise and scoop out the seeds with a teaspoon. Cut each piece in half again lengthwise, then in half crosswise.

■ Spread the cucumber out on a large plate. Sprinkle over the salt, then arrange the cucumber skin side up. Put another plate or chopping board on the cucumber and place a 2-pound weight, or a saucepan full of water, on top. Leave overnight.

■ Plunge the cucumber into cold water, then drain. Arrange the cucumber pieces side by side in a bundle. Take the bundle in your hands and squeeze out as much water as you can. With scissors, cut into bite-sized pieces about 1/2-inch long.

■ Cut off any discolored pieces from the ginger and grate.

■ In a bowl, mix together the cucumber pieces, grated ginger, soy sauce and *schichimi-togarashi*. The pickle is now ready to eat.

■ To store, refrigerate in a lidded container.

KYURI NO SOKUSEKI TSUKE MONO
■ INSTANT CUCUMBER PICKLE ■

SERVES 4

THIS AND the following recipe are a cross between Japanese pickles and salad. They don't have the intensity and bite of matured or even overnight pickles, but are an excellent alternative.

The first makes a crispy, salty accompaniment to plain, unsalted Japanese rice. Salt the cucumber before you start to cook the rice, then simply drain at the last minute.

1/2 cucumber   1 tablespoon salt

PEEL THE cucumber. Cut into quarters lengthwise and then into bite-sized pieces (about 1/2-inch).
■ Spread the cucumber pieces out on a plate and sprinkle with salt. Drain the cucumber just before serving.

KYURI NO SHOGA ZUKE
■ INSTANT GINGERED CUCUMBER PICKLE ■

SERVES 4

A MORE luxurious and flavorful version of the preceeding pickle. Use a young, tender piece of ginger as you will find it gives out more juice when grated and squeezed.

1/2 cucumber   3-inch piece fresh ginger root
1 tablespoon salt   1 teaspoon toasted sesame seeds

PEEL THE cucumber. Cut into quarters lengthwise and then into bite-sized pieces (about 1/2-inch).
■ Lay out on a plate and sprinkle with the salt.
■ Just before serving, drain the cucumber and toss with the sesame seeds. Grate the ginger, then scoop up in your hand and squeeze over the cucumber until it gives out no more juice.

DRINKS

JAPANESE TEA

■ O C H A ■

O utside Kyoto during the fresh golden spring days, tea pickers wearing traditional blue cotton working clothes and shady hats can be seen moving slowly across the ancient terraced tea hills, hand-picking the aromatic leaves. The youngest tips live a short but cosseted life in a cool, dappled, shady world sheltered from the direct sunlight by slatted bamboo blinds. Immediately after picking, the precious tips are steamed to destroy the enzymes that would otherwise turn their vivid green to brown. The result is Japan's most prized, and almost unaffordable, green leaf tea, *gyokuro*, which is used in an almost fresh state. The same first-picked tips are also ground into a brilliant emerald-green powder, *matcha*, which is used in the famous Japanese tea ceremony.

After the youngest tips have been harvested the bamboo blinds are removed and the next grade of tea is picked, *sencha*, which is made from the slightly larger leaves further down the stems. It is a very high-quality tea and is served on special occasions, or to special guests, and in the finest restaurants.

The next grade of tea is *bancha* which is composed of the lowest leaves and young twigs. This is the tea served in most Japanese restaurants. It is very refreshing and cleansing to the palate, contains less caffeine than the above teas and complements Japanese food.

The final cutting is a sort of pruning of the coarser twigs and stems to produce the lowest grade of tea, *kukicha*. It has a slightly earthy taste and when chilled makes a refreshing summer drink. It is very low in caffeine and is often given to children mixed with fruit juice.

Tea was introduced into Japan about 700 years ago by Buddhist monks who used it as a herbal remedy, tonic and mild stimulant. In the 13th century the tea ceremony was developed as a Zen Buddhist ritual, *cha-no-yu*. The perfection of the ceremony for both the preparer and receiver, ideally embodying the qualities of simplicity, beauty, appreciation, mutual respect, contentedness, harmony, purity and stillness, was considered one of the paths to enlightenment.

In the 17th century, many beautiful tea pavilions and tea houses were built, surrounded by traditional Japanese gardens of ideal natural beauty. Most of them are still flourishing today, offering a physical and spiritual space out of frenetic urban Japan, into a world of beauty, serenity and meditation.

Everyday tea drinking is a more casual affair. On visiting someone's house you are always offered green tea and cakes, and as you take your seat in a Japanese restaurant you are brought a small, woven basket containing a refreshing, damp, sometimes scented rolled towel, *oshibori*, which is either hot or chilled according to the season, and a bowl of *bancha* tea which is continuously refilled free of charge throughout the meal.

HOW TO MAKE JAPANESE TEA

The lowest grade of Japanese tea, *kukicha*, is boiled to release its flavor. Other green leaf teas are usually made as follows:

1. Warm a Japanese porcelain teapot, *kyusu*, and drinking bowls. Put 2 level teaspoons of tea leaves per person into the pot.

2. Bring some freshly drawn water to a boil. Allow it to cool a little (never use boiling water for Japanese tea). Pour the hot water over the leaves, filling the pot. Do not stir the tea.

3. Put the lid on the pot and allow the tea to infuse for 1-2 minutes.

4. Holding down the lid, pour the tea into the drinking bowls filling them about 2/3 full and completely emptying the teapot. Do not leave any liquid in the pot otherwise it will become bitter.

5. Refill the teapot with fresh hot water and continue as before, topping up the drinking bowls and refilling the pot as necessary. The teapot can be refilled with hot water 3 or 4 times before changing the leaves.

To drink the tea, pick up the drinking bowl with the fingers of your right hand, and while supporting it at the same time on the palm of your left hand, sip the tea. A slight slurping noise is usually made, especially if the tea is hot.

UMESHU
■ PLUM WINE ■

MAKES 5 1/2 PINTS

DURING MY first visit to my daughter-in-law Kaori's family home I was given a drink of uniquely delicious, sweet and fragrant Japanese plum wine, *umeshu*. It was served in a tiny shallow lacquered bowl gilded with plum blossoms which shimmered through the clear golden liquid.

Umeshu can be drunk at any time. It is sometimes taken as an aperitif, or on the rocks at the end of a meal. Some Japanese drink a tot before going to bed to ensure a good night's sleep.

Umeshu is simple to make and many Japanese women make 2 or 3 bottles each year to lay down for the following year. It is usually made from *shochu*, a Japanese spirit, and the green *ume shu* plum. Any variety of plum that is green when ripe can be used, but do not use sour, unripened plums. Select very fresh, firm undamaged plums.

■
2 1/2 pounds ripe green plums
3 1/2 sugar

■
8 cups *shochu* or vodka

■

■

CAREFULLY REMOVE the stalks and wash the plums without damaging them. Cover in cold water and leave to soak for 1 hour. Dry the plums thoroughly with a clean kitchen towel. Using a bamboo skewer or cocktail stick, prick each plum about 20 times all over.

■ Sterilize with boiling water a wide-topped lidded jar large enough to hold the plums and sugar, and dry it thoroughly.

■ Put a layer of plums on the bottom of the jar. Sprinkle over a good handful of sugar. Repeat until the jar is full, finishing with a layer of sugar. Pour the *shochu* over the plums to cover. Seal very tightly and leave in a cool, dark place for at least 6 months.

■ Umeshu can be drunk when the sugar has dissolved but it is best to leave it for 1 year.

To know the plums,
Look to your heart
And look to your nose.

ONISURA (1661-1738)

JAPANESE INGREDIENTS AND UTENSILS

Aburage Flat, rectangular sheets of dried soy bean curd, *tofu*. Usually sold in transparent packages of 3 sheets. Will keep well stored in an airtight container or plastic bag in the freezer.

Adzuki beans Small, red, slightly sweet beans, available in Japanese, Asian and health food shops. Will keep well stored in an airtight jar.

Ajitsuke-nori Small, wafer-thin strips of dried, seasoned *nori* seaweed with an intense seafood flavor. Usually sold in packages containing several small packets. Unopened packets keep well stored in an airtight container with the desiccant (moisture absorber) which came with the package.

Aonori-ko Powdered kelp seaweed available in Japanese and health food shops. Opened packages keep well in an airtight container.

Atsuage Chunky cubes, triangles or rectangles of deep-fried soy bean curd, *tofu*. Will keep for several months stored in an airtight container or plastic bag in the freezer.

Chopsticks (hashi) Japanese chopsticks are usually made of bamboo, plain or laquered wood and come in various lengths. The longer chopsticks are used for handling pieces of food when dipping into batter, frying, etc., for beating eggs and for mixing various ingredients. The shorter chopsticks are the only implements used to eat an entire Japanese meal, with the exception of savory custard, *chawan mushi*, which is eaten with a spoon.

Daikon Giant white radish 12-inches or more in length. Either cooked, sliced and eaten raw in salads, or grated and used as a garnish. Also obtainable in Indian food shops where it is known as *mooli*. Japanese *daikon* is also pickled; see *takuan*.

Dashi Clear soup stock (for details of various *dashis* see pages 29-30).

Donabe A small, earthenware, Lidded casserole glazed inside and out. It can be used over direct heat or in the oven.

Donburi See page 56.

Fu Small, dry, very absorbent pieces of feather-light starchy gluten (wheat protein) in various shapes. Usually floated on soups.

Furikake Seasoning garnish for rice (for details and recipes see pages 68-9).

Gohan Short-grained Japanese rice with a high gluten content. *Must* be used when specified in a recipe; in other recipes, although not so authentic, you can substitute your normal short-grain white rice.

Goma (sesame seeds) Both white and black. Black seeds have a slightly stronger flavor and are available in Japanese shops where they are sold natural or ready toasted. White sesame seeds are sold in Japanese, Chinese, Indian and health food stores. Before using untoasted seeds, either lightly toast, dry fry or bake in the oven, until they begin to jump. This will develop their rich, nutty flavor. Take care not to burn them or they will become bitter. Will keep well in an airtight container.

Hajikami-shoga Thin threads of red pickled ginger usually sold in flat, transparent plastic packages. Will keep well in an airtight container or plastic bag in the refrigerator.

Harusame (spring-rain) noodles Fine, translucent Japanese noodles made of potato or soy bean starch.

Hijiki Type of seaweed. Black-green firm-textured threads with a unique, rich flavor. Usually sold dried in transparent plastic packages. Available in Japanese and health food shops. Will keep well stored in an airtight container.

Karashi Japanese mustard. *Karashi* is almost identical to English mustard, but a little hotter. Available as powder which should be mixed into a paste with a little water, as required. Any leftover made mustard should be refrigerated and used within a few days. Also available ready made in tubes. English made mustard can be used as an alternative.

Kombu Kelp seaweed. Usually sold dried in strips in a transparent plastic package. Keeps well in an airtight container. Chinese kelp, *hai ts'ao*, can be used as an alternative.

Konnyaku Processed from the glutinous root of the devils tongue into either solid, gelatinous, brown/grey cakes or spaghetti-like threads, *ita-konnyaku*. Being calorie-free it is an excellent aid to dieting. *Konnyaku* is eaten in Japan to clear the digestive tract of toxins. Can be bought fresh or canned. Fresh *konnyaku* will keep for 3 days stored in an airtight container or plastic bag in the refrigerator.

Lotus root (renkon) Long, white, root vegetable. When sliced, a beautiful symmetrical pattern is revealed. Can be bought fresh, dried or canned. Fresh lotus root will keep for several days stored in an airtight container or plastic bag in the refrigerator.

Makisu Flexible bamboo rolling mat made of fine strips of bamboo held together by cotton string. It is used for rolling *sushi*, Japanese omelets and vegetables into a cylinder, the spaces between the strips allowing the moisture to escape. A slatted bamboo table mat can be substituted.

Matsutake Pine mushrooms. Available in the autumn from exotic mushroom farms in this country. They have a unique and distinctive flavor and slightly crisp texture. Will keep for about 3 days in a plastic bag in the refrigerator.

Mirin A very sweet, syrupy, Japanese rice wine used in cooking. An opened bottle will last several months. A syrup can be substituted made of 50 percent sugar dissolved in 50 perent water

Miso Richly flavored, fermented soy bean paste used as an ingredient in Japanese cooking and in *miso* soup. There are basically 4 types of *miso*: *shiru miso* is white and sweet; *inaka miso* is a golden color; *aka miso* or red *miso* is a reddish-chestnut color with a heavier flavor; and *sendai miso* is also a reddish chestnut color with a heavier salt content. Which *miso* you use for *miso* soup is mostly a matter of personal taste (see introduction to Thick Soups on page 40). *Miso* is usually sold in transparent plastic packages. It keeps well in an airtight container or plastic bag in the refrigerator.

Mochi Small, sticky savory rice cakes usually sold individually wrapped in plastic packages. Will last for several months in an airtight container or plastic bag in the freezer.

Mochi-gome Very glutinous short-grained rice used for making sticky red rice, *sekihan*, and sticky rice cakes, *mochi*.

Natto Soy beans fermented in malt. Usually sold in small, individual plastic packages that also contain a tiny packet of Japanese mustard. Will last several days stored in an airtight container or plastic bag in the refrigerator.

Nori Black-green laver seaweed which is pressed and dried into paper-thin sheets, with a delicious seafood flavor. Usually sold in flat tins or transparent plastic packages. Opened packages keep well stored in an airtight container with the desiccant (moisture absorber) that came with the package.

Ramen Type of noodles made from wheat flour, available dried. Instant *ramen* noodles are also available. These come in individual packages containing packets of instant soup base powder. Japanese instant *ramen* noodles are preferable, but Taiwanese brands, available in Asian food shops, are very good.

Sake A potent, fortified Japanese rice wine. Both drinking and cooking *sake*, which is a little cheaper, can be used for cooking. Keeps well if, after opening, you replace stopper and refrigerate.

Schichimi-togarashi *Schichimi* means seven different, and *togarashi* means pepper. This Japanese seven-spice pepper seasoning can include, according to the particular manufacturer, sesame, poppy, rape and hemp seeds, flaked red peppers, flaked *nori* seaweed, ground brown *sansho* pods, and dried citrus peel. Used sprinkled over noodles and rice dishes. Will last several months stored in an airtight container.

Sesame seeds See *goma*.

Shamoji Small, flat bamboo or wooden paddle used to turn over hot, cooked rice allowing the steam to escape; also used for serving rice. Rice will not stick to a *shamoji* as much as to a metal spoon. A flat wooden spatula or spoon may be substituted.

Shiitake Type of mushroom frequently used in Japanese cooking, either dry or fresh. Fresh *shiitakes* are obtainable from most of the larger supermarkets or from exotic mushroom farms and will last for a few days stored in an airtight container or plastic bag in the refrigerator. Dried *shiitakes* keep well stored in an airtight container. Oyster mushrooms can be used as an alternative.

Shirataki White, spaghetti-like threads processed from the root of the *konnyaku* or devils tongue. Being calorie-free, *shirataki* is an excellent aid to slimming.

Shochu A 40% distilled alcohol used for making *Umeshu*, plum wine. Vodka can be substituted.

Shoga-ama-zuke Thin slices of pink, pickled ginger usually sold in transparent, flat plastic packages. A Korean version known as *gung-chua*, which is obtainable in most Asian food shops, can be substituted. The Korean version is white and therefore doesn't make such an attractive garnish as the pink Japanese ginger, but it tastes almost identical. Once opened, will last for several months stored in an airtight container in the refrigerator.

Shoyu Japanese soy sauce naturally brewed from soy beans and wheat. Dark soy sauce, *koikuchi-shoyu*, is the most commonly used in Japan for general cooking purposes and is also served as a condiment at every meal. The Japanese brand Kikkoman dark soy sauce was used in the recipes in this book containing soy sauce. Alternatively, light-colored soy sauce, *usutuchishoyu*, can be used to avoid coloring a pale-colored dish. It is a little saltier than dark soy sauce and lacks its richness of aroma and flavor. *Tamari* is heavier, darker and richer than dark soy sauce and is sometimes used as a dip. If not available, Chinese "thin" soy sauce, which is not so authentic, can be substituted for Japanese dark soy sauce. Once opened, soy sauce will last for about 18 months if stored in a plastic bottle, or 2 years if stored in a glass bottle, after which its flavor and aroma will begin to deteriorate.

Soba Japanese brown noodles made from buckwheat flour. The buckwheat noodles obtainable in health food shops can be substituted.

Somen Fine, white Japanese noodles made from wheat flour.

Soy sauce See *shoyu*.

Soy beans (daizu) Small, round, cream-colored beans sold in Japanese, Asian and health food shops. Keep well stored in an airtight can.

Su Japanese vinegar made from distilled rice wine, with a delicate, slightly sweet flavor. Used in salads and sweet-and sour dishes. Chinese rice vinegar or diluted cider vinegar can be used as an alternative. Keeps well stored in a cool, dark place.

Suribashi Japanese pestle and mortar. The earthenware bowl is serrated inside to aid grinding or pulverizing with the wooden pestle.

Sushi See page 59.

Sushi-su Similar to *su* vinegar, but should be used when making sweet-vinegared rice, *sushi*.

Takenoko Bamboo shoots, either fresh or canned. Also available in Chinese food shops where they are known as *choksun*. Fresh bamboo shoots will last for several days stored in an airtight container or plastic bag in the refrigerator.

Takuan Bright yellow, strongly flavored pickled giant radish, *daikon*, about 12-inches in length. To serve, cut into slices and cut each slice into 4 pieces. Also grated and used in various recipes. Keeps well in an airtight container or plastic bag in the refrigerator.

Tamago yoki nabe Small, rectangular frying pan used for making perfect, rectangular rolled omelets. A small, round frying pan, *oyako-nabe,* is occasionally used for making omelets.

Tempura-tsuyu Clear dipping sauce for vegetables in a golden batter, *tempura.* Either make your own (see page 121) or purchase ready made. I always use the brand name "Yamasa" *tempura-tsuya* as it doesn't contain any animal products and is very delicious.

Tofu Soy bean curd. Available in health food, Japanese and Chinese food shops, and many supermarkets. It is made by straining soy bean "milk" through either cotton or silk. The milk is then coagulated and pressed to form a block. Straining through cotton produces the firm *momen-dofu* or cotton *tofu* which is the most widely available and commonly used. Unless otherwise stated, this is the *tofu* used in all recipes requiring fresh *tofu*. The fresh cotton *tofu* sold in Asian food shops is usually packageed floating in water in a plastic carton. It will last up to one week in the refrigerator if you put it in an airtight container, cover with cold water in which a good pinch of salt has been dissolved and cover tightly. The water should be changed every day. Before use, cotton *tofu* is usually drained of excess water, which allows the stock or soup in which it is simmered to penetrate and flavor the *tofu*. To drain, wrap the *tofu* in a clean kitchen towel and leave to drain for about 30 minutes. Purists would leave the wrapped *tofu* between 2 boards to facilitate drainage, but I don't always do this. The cotton *tofu* available in health food shops is less delicate than that sold in Asian shops and needs less draining. Although not as authentic, it makes a reasonably satisfactory substitute. It is usually sold in sealed plastic packages. Unopened packages should be kept in the refrigerator and used by the sell-by date on the carton. Naturally smoked *tofu*, which has a salty, bacony flavor, is also available in health food shops in similar cartons and is quite useful to add to Japanese dishes that would contain small pieces of ham. Straining soy milk through silk before coagulating produces *kinu-goshi* or silken *tofu*. It comes in 2 varieties, one slightly firmer than the other. I have used the firmer variety in the recipes. They are both very delicate with a consistency similar to a light egg custard. They are usually sold in long-lasting packages that look rather like small cartons of UHT milk. Unopened cartons should be kept in the refrigerator and used by the sell-by date on the carton.

Tonkatsu sauce A spicy brown sauce, a little thinner than, but very similar to, English brown sauce, such as H.P., from which it was derived, and which can be used instead.

Tororo-kombu Pale green skeins of soft, kelp seaweed shavings, with a strong, slightly vinegar flavor. Usually sold in transparent plastic packages. Keeps well stored in an airtight container or plastic bag in the refrigerator.

Tsuke mono Japanese pickles. Either make your own (see pages 146-50) or select from the many excellent, commercially prepared varieties that are sold in plastic packages and are available from Japanese and some Asian food shops, such as pickled sour plums, cucumber, pink ginger, radish, eggplants, etc. It is nice to have a selection on the table at a Japanese meal for the diners to select their favorite. Opened packages will keep well in the refrigerator either in an airtight container, or fold over the top of the plastic package and secure with an elastic band.

Udon Thick, white Japanese noodles made from wheat flour. Available dried, or partly cooked in plastic packages containing a packet of instant soup base powder. Unopened packages of the partly cooked variety keep well in the refrigerator.

Umeboshi Deep pink, pickled plums with an intensely plumy, sweet-and-sour flavor. Also in available in tubes as *umeboshi* paste. Eaten as a pickle with plain rice or mashed and used in various dishes. Chinese pickled sour plums in brine can be used as an alternative.

Vegetable oil The Japanese use refined vegetable oils to fry food rather than animal fat. The most commonly used oils are refined sunflower, safflower, rapeseed or corn oil, such as those obtainable in most supermarkets, the criteria being that they can withstand cooking at high temperatures, and also that they do not impart a marked flavor of their own to the food. If a stronger flavor is required, a little sesame oil is mixed with the vegetable oil.

Vinegar, Japanese See *su* and *sushi-su.*

Wakame Type of seaweed, bright green with a delicate texture. Sold dried in plastic packages containing several packets of ready trimmed and cut *wakame,* or in a long, dried strip. Once opened, will keep well in an airtight container or plastic bag, in the refrigerator.

Wasabi Japanese horseradish. A bright green, hot and fragrant condiment made from the grated or powdered root of the *wasabia japonica.* Fresh *wasabi* roots are difficult to obtain in this country. Use ready mixed *wasabi* paste in tubes, or powdered *wasabi* sold in small cans to mix into a paste with water as required. Leftover made *wasabi* should be refrigerated and used within a few days.

Yuzu Japanese citrus fruit. The fragrant rind is grated and sprinkled over soups and other dishes. Although not quite so authentic, lemon, lime or seville orange peel may be substituted.

SUPPLIERS OF JAPANESE FOOD

The ingredients used in this book can all be found in markets featuring the foods of Japan. Many of them can also be found in markets featuring Asian foods, as well as any well-stocked supermarket. Ingredients not found locally may be available from the mail-order markets listed below.

Adriana's Caravan
409 Vanderbilt Street
Brooklyn, NY 11218
800-316-0820 or 718-436-8565

Frieda's-By-Mail
Frieda's Inc.
4465 Corporate Center Drive
Los Alamitos, CA 90720-2561
800-241-1771

Gourmail, Inc.
816 Newton Road
Berwyn, PA 19312
215-296-4620

House of Spices
76-17 Broadway
Jackson Heights
Queens, NY 11373
718-507-4900

Nancy's Specialty Market
P.O. Box 1302
Stamford, CT 06904
800-462-6291

Oriental Food Market and Cooking School
2801 Howard Street
Chicago, IL 60645
312-274-2826

Oriental Market
502 Pampas Drive
Austin, TX 78752
512-453-9058

Pacific Mercantile Company, Inc.
1925 Lawrence Street
Denver, CO 80202
303-295-0293

Rafal Spice Company
2521 Russell Street
Detroit, MI 48207
313-259-6373

Uwajimaya
P.O. Box 3003
Seattle, WA 98114
206-624-6248

Vietnam Imports
922 W. Broad Street
Falls Church, VA 22046
703-534-9941

INDEX

Vegetarian Cookbooks by The Crossing Press

Low-Fat Vegetarian Cooking: Classic Slim Cuisine
By Sue Kreitzman

Adapting popular vegetarian dishes from the cuisines of the world, Master chef Sue Kreitzman has created more than 100 new low-fat or non-fat dishes for vegetarians and anyone wanting to reduce the fat in their diets. With this collection, eating a healthful diet does not mean skimping on flavor.

6 X 9 • 208pp • $14.95 • Paper • ISBN 0-89594-834-6

Mother Nature's Garden: Healthy Vegan Cooking
By Florence and Mickey Bienenfeld

In addition to eliminating animal products, including eggs and dairy, these 400 vegan recipes are low in fat and salt, cholesterol-free and sugar-free. Includes breakfast and brunch specialties, soups, appetizers, entrees, and festive holiday dishes. "If you want to eat healthier, but still want that homey old world taste, this book could make you happy." —*Vegetarian Times*

8 1/8 x 9 • 234pp • $14.95 • Paper • ISBN 0-89594-702-1

The Spice Box: Vegetarian Indian Cookbook
By Manju Shivraj Singh

"I strongly recommend *The Spice Box* ... Recipes for the most part are simple and straightforward, but the end results would never reveal the simplicity of the food's preparation." —*Vegetarian Times*

6 x 8 7/8 • 222pp • $12.95 • Paper • ISBN 0-89594-053-1

International Vegetarian Cooking
By Judy Ridgway

International Vegetarian Cooking presents more than 400 new vegetarian dishes adapted from the world's most popular cuisines and outlines dietary guidelines, offers tips for successful menu planning, gives time-saving suggestions, and provides ideas for special occasions and parties.

6 X 9 • 192pp • $14.95 • Paper • ISBN 0-89594-854-0

To receive a current catalog from The Crossing Press,
please call toll-free,
800-777-1048.
Visit our Website on the Internet at: www.crossingpress.com